EVERYTHING HAPPENED
IN VIETNAM

THE YEAR OF THE RAT

by

Robert Peter Thompson

BLUE MOON PUBLISHING

Published by Blue Moon Publishing

13640 Elkwood Drive, Apple Valley, MN 55124-8774

c/o Robert P. Thompson

The incidents and events described within this book are true stories based upon the recollections of the author. Some of the names have been changed . Nicknames such as "Tater" and "Sandy" are the actual nicknames of the persons described. Names of designated units, places and locations are reconstructed to the best of my memory. This is not a work of fiction although I have written it more like a novel than a narrative. I have thought that perhaps it could be called true fiction because it has more of the feel of a novel. However, in the final chapter there is an event concerning Sandy, myself and the "Big Bird" that may not be digestible as literal truth. Although it is for the author. The reader will have to decide for his or herself.

Visit My Site: www.everythinghappenedinvietnam.com

ISBN: 978-0-6152-4498-3

~ But not everything is remembered and not everything is told. Lost with those who did not survive and with those who did not return. Lost in the chaos and confusion and the self protective suppression of the formidable and yet fragile mind. Sometimes that which affects you most is that which you can no longer see and is perhaps better left alone. But what of that which so stubbornly remains and cries out as it does from the darkness of time and says:

"I am here, I am still here, you will look at me, for I will never go away."

The author

For Sandy

CONTENTS

THE RAT

It's impossible to recreate. The wet fermented air pressed heavily on my sweating chest and face. Bare from the waist up, collapsed on my back in the trench, my whole body felt weighted against the slash in the red dirt. The trench ran the perimeter of our compound linking the lookout bunkers and the silent bleary eyed Marines who stared at and listened to the restless blackness of another sweltering Southeast Asian night. Still on high alert, I slept close to the bunker but not in it. You could breathe better outside and the trench was less of a target. Sleep had been hard to come by for the last couple of weeks and the numbing exhaustion weighed against the flood of tension unleashed by recent events.

Especially during the darkest hours. The black time. When the sudden pop of an illumination flare jolts your sinking consciousness back into a frenzied focus. Treading frantically on the surface of a malevolent sea of dancing light and shadows. Trying in vain to separate the real from the imagined amidst the macabre interplay of swinging parachute flare and the resulting movement of objects stationary and not so stationary, as the sputtering flare of light slowly settles and is swallowed by its dark master.

None of us who remained would ever be the same. Nor of course would those who had gone. Even the landscape had changed. Rings of razor sharp concertina wire encircled our two breast shaped mounds where before only a barbed wire fence had run. Trip flares and tangle wire complimented the spiral barriers we had been installing with such sweaty urgency. A task for which it was my good fortune to be assigned as the driver of the truck. An ancient relic from some past forgotten war that bravely lurched and grinded along the edge of the recently abandoned rice paddies surrounding our camp. Many of the hooches had disappeared, including my own. Reduced to black cinder smudges against the red ground. Nothing left but the shadow. But mostly what changed was our outlook. Our outward attention was suddenly intensified profoundly. As if God himself had reached down and grabbed us by the collective throat.

For me though and for now, God's fingers were slowly relaxing their grip and my struggle to concentrate was coming to a blissful and effortless end, as I sank gratefully into the arms of an irresistible dreamless sleep. Relieved of the watch by my reluctant replacement and to the comforting cadence of his unraveling string of poetic profanity, I let go of the outward and fell in like a rock.

Sometime during those early morning hours, between the changing of the watch and first light, a lone Marine lieutenant walked along the perimeter checking the lookouts and those on watch, pausing briefly at each bunker for a whispered word of encouragement or levity, anything to boost alertness.

Sleep! Cool, black, effortless sleep. Of course I didn't hear him coming. And I didn't budge when the Lieutenant came to a stop and found Alverez, who had taken the watch, alert and in good verbal form, which drew a muffled chuckle from the LT who I had, as of yet, never seen before in my life.

No, I was sprawled out flat on my back against the steep slope of the chevron shaped trench. Arms splayed out dejectedly to my sides. Unmoved since the moment my upper eyelids slammed down on their respective lower mates. And if it wasn't for the pop of a new flare, which I also did not hear and its resulting ghostly light, which I did not see, then the Lieutenant would not have seen, nor come scrambling down the trench and attempt to dislodge with the full force thrust of his boot, what was sitting on my bare still sweating chest. And if the Lieutenant in his enraged and scrambling haste, propelled I am sure by the enormous blasphemy to the Corps his eyes in quivering flare light beheld, had not missed in entirety the loathsome and malignant creature hideously perched upon my chest and had not instead landed the hard toe of his regulation size ten and one half tropical jungle boot squarely against my upper right side rib cage with the equivalent sudden impact of a 105 millimeter artillery round, then my hitherto slumbering eyelids would not have burst open wide in unguarded wonderment. Only to be filled with -- strike that -- optically raped by, in the quaking strobe light of the sputtering flare, the permanently frozen transfixed image of utterly godless black and beady eyes. Hideously extended cadaverous death grin teeth and forward fangs protruding with menace and evil intent through oily taut stretched lips and raised, ready to strike, quivering flexed out claws exactly right smack dab in my face. Only for an instant.

The Rat.

I can still feel the repulsive impressions of its cool clammy feet even to this day.

Oh, and by the way, this was no ordinary rat. This was the biggest, filthiest, monstrous rat that you would never want to see. As big as any city full grown house fed cat on the upside. And one other thing. The very very first thought I was able to assemble, even before the Lieutenant's boot had fully recoiled from its explosive insult to my naked unprotected rib cage and as the Rat hurled airborne sideways to my left toward its old and always dark half-sunk culvert lair, I recalled the thought. Actually the knowledge of an ugly awareness that had seeped into my exposed and opened brain not too many days or nights or some kind of time before. And that is, the way things happened, the way that guys were killed and wounded, I mean you could never find all of the pieces. Not all of them. Right there in the red dirt. Mixed in with the sand and shreds and fragments of sand bags and blown bunkers. Underneath things in the trench and in the culvert. In the darkness, with the Rat.

The Rat had found and eaten parts of guys I knew. Guys I worked with. Bullshitted with. Guys I had laughed with, drank with, smoked with or tried to ignore. A guy I had just met the night before it happened. I mean the night that it began. You see I knew that the Rat, immediately before the boot, before my eyes flew open and I saw... Only for an instant. The eyes, face, mouth and claws of fully fledged rat expression magnified to the size of a drive-in movie screen. It was that close. I knew and I could somehow feel the lingering presence of the Rat's lips close to the point of touching my own then slightly open, slow breathing, deep sleeping mouth. And I also knew that it wasn't about to kiss me.

Everything happened in Vietnam. Not to me but to someone or something. Everything happened. For some it was the Year of the Monkey. For some it was the Year of the Dog. But regardless of the Chinese calendar, for me it was the Year of the Rat.

CAPTAIN SMILEY

I remember the day I met Captain Smiley. Well he wasn't a Captain yet but he soon would be. He was coming down the little dirt road with a driver and a jeep from Danang. The road, not much more than a rice paddy dike, came from another slightly bigger dirt road that headed north through Da Lai Pass. The Pass cut through the steep razor-ridged mountains that ran around the north and west sides of our camp. I call them mountains, even though they are in all probability classified as hills, because I'm from Minnesota and because of the patrols we humped up and down the steep accordion like ravines that drained from the crest. Things are always bigger when you are up close.

Anyway, Captain Smiley's jeep is kicking up a cloud of dust coming down the road just as I was coming in from a sweep of what used to be rice paddies and the scrub bush area between our wire and the ridge. The thing is and what captured my attention, aside from the mortar rounds exploding on either side of the road behind Smiley's jeep, punctuating the plume of red dust rising like a rooster tail in its wake and aside from the shit-faced expression of the now pedal-to-the-metal, white knuckle, fish tailing driver from Danang, was the splendid repose of Captain Smiley.

Hands comfortably clasped behind his head. Right leg fully extended up and over the front seat passenger door. And pipe confidently clenched in his United States Marine Corps mandibles in a manner that would have put General Mac Arthur to shame. If they were trying to send Captain Smiley a message, he sure as hell wasn't giving them any satisfaction. His indifference to the escort of exploding mortar rounds walking zigzag behind the jeep was truly stunning. He might as well have been spending a pleasant afternoon on the lake pulling a water skier, whose successive slalom turns kick up a tuft of white spray along either side of a line behind the boat. The plumes of white smoke and dust lifted into the air by the explosions of the mortars lingered briefly, curled over and were dispersed by the gentle breeze. Just as the harried driver and the jeep from Danang were seemingly there one moment, turned and were gone with the wind. Leaving Captain Smiley, his sea bag and only myself standing there to greet him as the dust of the departed jeep blew over and settled to the ground about our feet.

Which brings me to the very first words I heard uttered by the seemingly implacable Captain Smiley. No, not a word about being chased by the errant efforts of a North Vietnamese Army mortar man down our long little driveway from the main dirt road. That he appeared to accept as if it were pre-planned. An incendiary entourage assembled temporarily simply to accentuate the occasion of his arrival. What brought Captain Smiley to speak and the issue of his immediate concern was the appearance of the nineteen-year-old Marine lance corporal, soon to be corporal, who stood in rapt amazement before him. You see what I was wearing and what I wasn't wearing for the past four or five days and nights or some kind of time prior to his arrival, as I stood there mute as a statue before him, was a helmet, flak jacket, utility belt and magazines, my M16 rifle, two extra bandoleers of ammunition and a pair of faded olive drab regulation Marine Corps boxer shorts that had seen their better days. In fact, the only actual item of clothing was the green skivvies. No shirt, no trousers, no socks and no boots. Just the dirt, mud and slime, still dripping down my legs from the sweep patrol of what used to be rice paddies, just outside of the wire. In the face of such impropriety and with a voice heavy on exasperation, but also with an apparently genuine concern, Captain Smiley, who like the saltiest of surfers, had just ridden in on a wave of exploding mortar rounds, inquired to his still speechless audience of one: "Goddamit Marine! Where in the hell are your boots?"

Somewhat surprised by this line of inquiry and as he pulled from his sea bag and pitched a pair of brand new size ten, green canvas topped jungle boots in my direction, all that I could do was point lamely to the large black smudge ten feet behind and to the right, where my hooch used to be.

I don't know precisely what it was that was special about Captain Smiley. Perhaps it was only special to me. A sort of brightness. The kind of brightness that Sandy had. Sandy was the battalion mailman. He brought letters and packages from the World to our camp and to the other artillery batteries in the battalion. It was a very enviable job but no one could have done it better than Sandy. Everybody liked him and not just because of the letters and packages, because not everybody got those, but what everybody got when Sandy popped in was a burst of light. You didn't have to ask about the name when you saw him. You knew right away it was because of his hair. A sandy blond shag of surfer hair and a smile that looked like it had just rolled in on a sun crested wave from the California coast.

Sandy would serve out his tour of duty to the very last day, but the wave would not return and would be remembered always at full crest. Tinged with light, with promise and forever young.

Captain Smiley on the other hand was up there. Not as old as the guy he was replacing, but late twenties, early thirties, easy. The old man he was replacing was a real decent guy. An old salt. But all of a sudden he wasn't there anymore. He wasn't killed. He was just gone. I never was sure what happened. Maybe it was because he was next to the staff sergeants' hooch. They all got blown to hell. Or maybe his hitch was up. I never really knew. He was just gone.

Captain Smiley, though, had arrived and in splendid style. He was the new S1 Admin Officer of Headquarters Battery, 1st Battalion, 13th Marines, 1st Marine Division, an artillery battalion. And I, barefoot and hoochless, was his sometimes service records book and correspondence clerk, who had been given, previous to his arrival, the perhaps unusual dual assignment of Squad Leader of our units Reaction Force. Twelve to fifteen Marines whose function was to congregate in the trench at the top of the hill which encompassed our compound. That is, whenever our camp was in the process or in danger of being hit. Whether by rockets, mortars, or by ground penetration, or all of the above, the

Corporal of the Guard, who was in radio communication with the perimeter posts, would, when aware of imminent threat, begin to turn the rotary lever on a hand cranked siren alarm. Which would initiate an amplified sound, whose pitch at the lowest decibels was akin to the wailing lamentations of a chorus of dry-throated sinners in the wretched bowels of hell. But would rise with frenzy and velocity to a fevered pitch at the highest decibels, to a sound describable and remembered, only by imagination, as the agonized scream and tormented rage of a male fire-blowing dragon, whose testicles are being slowly crushed by the constriction of a pair of gigantic pliers.

I am sure that even to this day, anyone who truly experienced this sound, if heard in their dreams tonight, would pop out of bed like spit on a frying pan of boiling oil. Anyway, this was our signal to meet up in the trench, but it didn't always work out that way.

WE WEREN'T ALL HEROES

(8 WEEKS EARLIER)

Sometimes it seems that a string of words in a simple declaration had to have been crafted and then inserted into the lexicon of human utterances with a mischievous, if not malevolent intent, by a greater power.

A divinity, perhaps construed only by ourselves, to find macabre enjoyment in the foibles and failings of us mortal prisoners of the human cartoon. And so it seemed to me, when just a short time later, I reflected on the echo of the words expelled from the lips of a salty looking Marine, clad in tropical tiger shorts and perched on the wooden steps of the S1 Hooch,

23

as I arrived alone to report for duty to Headquarters Battery, 1st Battalion, 13th Marines:

"Welcome to Camp Henderson. This place hasn't been hit in over four years!"

Now this was the end of December, 1968, and a hell of a lot of war had already occurred and I also knew that as a Marine, I had volunteered. Which in my own brilliant way is how I avoided the draft. But I did not request to go to the two weeks of administration school after infantry training and I had already heard too many times what was said about Marines who begged out of some kind of cushy job for the infantry, only to end up with their legs blown off or to go home in a bag.

And it wasn't very complimentary. It usually went something like this:

"Dumb fucker. The dumb ass sonuvabitch got what he deserved. Fuckin A man. You shouldn't fuck with fate."

This followed by grunts of concurrence all the way around.

Fate! That was my True North. Right, wrong, good, bad or ugly. That was the only ball that I was going to keep my eye on. I would do whatever was asked of me and I felt some guilt at my good fortune. But whatever my fate would be, I didn't want anybody to say I was stupid.

Oh yeah, the guy in the tiger shorts? I don't think I ever saw him again. Must have been short and gone back to the World. Maybe I was replacing him. Or maybe he was only there to deliver his welcome and then like an apparition -- poof!

And so there I was. The sight, smell and feel of Vietnam hadn't really caught up with me yet. I had been up all night and it all seemed like a blur. The night ride down from Okinawa in a wind whistling rattley old C130, with the sea bags piled up in the middle and a couple of hundred unusually quiet Marines, lost in a state of frozen self analysis, plastered cheek-to-cheek on the plain wooden benching against both sides of the cavernous aircraft, had passed like a dream.

A dream I was shaken out of by the abrupt and bumpy touchdown of the old C130 on the tarmac of the airbase by Danang. Just as suddenly as the old bird had come to rest, the massive rear mouth of the plane began to open and something unforgettable happened.

Before we even began to disembark and as the monstrous steel lips of the loading bay began to part, the whole belly of the old plane seemed to constrict and then expand abruptly, as a rush of unearthly hot fetid heavy steam engulfed the entire hold. You could hear the collective groan as the shocked lungs of the new arrivals first rejected and then reluctantly inhaled their first breath of Vietnam. Of what would have to suffice as air.

But there was no time to contemplate our adjustment to this unwelcomed acclimation. At least not for myself and one other unfortunate *volunteer*. For as soon as the gang plank at the rear of the old airship touched the tarmac, a harried and impatient voice from the outer darkness was bellowing: "Let's go, let's go, let's go."

And the steam breathing occupants of the ancient air beast began in turn to stumble bravely into the heart of their own irrepressible darkness. That is all of us but two, who while spilling double file from the maw of the great beast, just like everybody else, were unexpectedly culled from the herd with a quick grab of our olive drab

26

shirt sleeves by the hands of the bellowing voice: "You two privates. Unload the sea bags. The rest of you. Move it! Move it! Move it! This airfield is a magnet for rockets!"

Now this is where I have to say a few things about good intentions. You see, about five months earlier, I was plucked out of my staging battalion in Okinawa on my way to Vietnam. We went from California to Hawaii where we spent two hours imprisoned in a high walled-in courtyard off the airport terminal, where you could hear the luscious sounds of the wind rustling the fronds of the palm trees and the rhythmic rise and fall of the waves against the moonlit sands of the beach, but you couldn't actually see any of it. Just the wall and a bunch of other restless, plotting, dreaming of escaping Marines. Trapped in a halfway place. Inches from paradise. In a holding pen. In transit to Vietnam.

As a battalion, we had spent the last month or so training together in the hills of Camp Pendleton, California. And we were on our way to Okinawa. Where we would spend only two days being processed and given orders for our new duty stations and assignments in the Republic of Vietnam. But then the inexplicable happened. Touchdown on a commercial airliner at Kadena Air Base on the island of Okinawa, in the East China Sea. A quick bus ride up to Camp Hansen Marine Base, 9th Marine Amphibious Brigade, for processing in transit *going south*. That's the way they said it in Okinawa. If you were going to Vietnam, you were: "Going South."

Anyway, after reporting in with everybody else and going through a bunch of bullshit, someone comes around asking for Private First Class PFC Thompson and that's me and so I go with him and I get reassigned to Camp Hansen, Okinawa as a Court Reporter, for which I never had one second of training. But under the able tutelage of "Chief", a Native American Marine, who *was* trained as a Court Reporter and who left me with a backlog of twenty untouched Dictaphone tape recordings of Courts Martial. That's how you say it. Courts Martial. You think it would be Court Martials. Plural. But it's not. It's Courts Martial. Anyway, they were garbled. Like in a foreign language. And Chief was a great guy but he was gone, and so I learned to record the trials by reporting them word for word into the mask of the Dictaphone and identifying the speaker and the participants: The five officers of the Court. The Accused and the opposing counsels of the Prosecution and Defense.

And it was five months of long nights and the backlog and the neon wonderland of Kin Village and the successful old mamason of a fine house with three tongues of fire on a sign over the door, who liked Japanese wrestling and let me watch, sitting cross legged on the mat on the floor and reminded me of my grandmother.

Until the day with the new law officer and the tapes in my hand. The tapes of my last case. The case of the nineteen year old Corporal. Good rank for his age and time in the Corps. Good behavior. Good Marine. Anyway, his mother has a serious stroke. So he goes home for a ten day emergency leave.

At the end of the ten days, she's still in the hospital and not doing very well, and the Corporal asks for and is granted a five day extension on his emergency leave. His request is granted, but during the five days, his mother who is still in the hospital has another stroke, which the Counsel for the Defense emphasizes is usually fatal. So the Corporal asks for a second five day extension of his emergency leave, but this time it is denied. It is explained by the Prosecution that the regulation under these circumstances only allows for one five day extension of a ten day emergency leave and the Corporal did not return by the fifth day of his five day extension and did not return, in fact, until three days after the fifth day of the five day extension, although on his own recognizance, as soon as his mother began to show improvement. And for this he was tried and convicted by Court Martial and sentenced to loss of rank from Corporal, E4, to Private, E1 and to imprisonment for a period of six months, as well as forfeiture of all pay and allowances. The six months imprisonment to be considered as *bad time.* To be made up on his enlistment upon completion of sentence.

Now in boot camp, at Marine Corps Recruit Depot, San Diego, we once crawled across the entire parade deck on our bellies. Across a massive field of asphalt. Pulled out our billfolds and pictures of our girl friends, family, mothers, whatever you had, and while we were ordered to look up at the flag from our prone maggot-like posture and then down at our pictures in repetitive fashion, the DI, at the top of his lungs, informed us how because of our unforgivable weakness, our mothers and girlfriends, for those who actually had girlfriends, would be raped and horribly murdered by godless communists. We were required to write our mothers at least once a week throughout boot camp.

Mothers are revered by the Corps. So I threw the tapes down on the new Captain's desk and I said: "I'm not going to have a damn thing more to do with this case." And I was right. The next day I was on a C130 *going south*.

Which brings me back to the lesson on good intentions. Although I had been promoted to Lance Corporal while I was still stationed in Okinawa, I wasn't wearing any chevrons on my collar when the hand of the bellowing voice grabbed my sleeve and the voice said: "You two privates." I had taken them off for the brilliant reason of not wanting to throw any rank around on guys that were already there when I got to Vietnam. It seemed like the right thing to do. So I got to unload two hundred, stuffed to the gills,

31

green Marine sea bags with my partner, as our lungs learned to live on the steam of truly tropical air.

The sweaty work didn't relieve all of the tension of waiting until sunrise and a ride out from Danang to wherever I was going, but it broke the ice.

From there it was the back bed of a six-by truck with a dozen other new replacements through the outskirts of the just awakening city of Danang and then out into the alien countryside at a high rate of speed. Everything flying by fast and intense. Impressions being formed by flashing observations. Kids along the side of the road in the relatively safe confines of the city, hollering for handouts and brazenly flipping us the bird, as we roared by. Kids in the more dangerous and isolated countryside waving, showing the peace or victory sign and shouting: "Marines number one." This time with a different finger extended and a hand painted sign by a ramshackle hut on the side of the road, that said: *Ice For Sell.*

As we barreled down unfamiliar roads, away from the city, a lingering image kept popping in my mind. Back in Danang, amidst the hustle of early morning street activity and out of the crowd as we rumbled by, I saw, only for a fleeting moment, what would remain forever impressed within my mind.

The most beautiful girl in the world.

I knew immediately that she was the offspring of a French and Vietnamese union. And I could see as well, in the aura of her angelic expression, a sense of inescapable sorrow and longing. As if she were a beautiful fragile flower, out of place and unwanted. And she seemed to be looking right at me.

Only for a moment. Never to be seen again.

But now in the countryside, the colorful dress and style of the city had turned to conical hats, loose fitting smock-like shirts and baggy black pajama-like pants. A generic and more rugged appearance. And while the image of the most beautiful girl in the world kept reprinting in my brain, I wondered just when and where somebody off the side of the road would start shooting at us.

THE YEAR OF THE RAT

Local children – The author – The Como Bunker

The Road out of Da Lai Pass

THE YEAR OF THE RAT

"IT DON'T MEAN NOTHIN"

The first seven weeks or so were relatively uneventful. People went about their business. Some of the older salts, that is those who had been in Country the longest, would occasionally open up and reveal personal experiences, giving us office pogues, supply clerks, transport types and what have you, a glimpse of the history of the First Battalion, Thirteenth Marines and the part our unit had played in the long saga of the Second Indochina War, that what would later be seen as a long battle in the fifty-years war against Communism.

These testimonials ranged from the siege of Khe Sanh, to the time when Alpha Battery was almost overrun, to the fall of Hue, the Imperial capital of Old Vietnam. In the early part of 1969 there were still Marines in our outfit who had survived all of these battles. These stories, as opposed to what you might expect, were not freely shared and the way that I heard of them is when some of us were sequestered before dawn to participate in certain field missions, such as providing security to a doctor and interpreter on MEDCAPs*. This is when a half dozen or so Marines would accompany a doctor to an outlying village to provide medical assistance to the villagers for various ailments, such as respiratory infections, broken bones, skin lesions, tapeworm and a host of other tropical diseases.

Other times, we would form up for routine search patrols of the area immediately surrounding our compound. We would meet at the commo bunker. You were usually never allowed to step foot inside this heavily fortified underground bunker and few people seemed to know what exactly went on in there, but on at least one occasion, when we were waiting to move

*(MEDCAP - Medical Civilian Assistance Program)

out and while it was still dark, I managed to slip inside and caught my very first look at what is now so commonplace - Cathode Ray Terminals. CRTs. The computer screens glowing an eerie green light in the otherwise dark and dank sand-bagged cave. Running solely on the juice of a gas powered generator.

Listening to these stories in the pre-dawn darkness by the commo bunker left an indelible mark. The cannon cocker from the long siege at Khe Sanh, surrounded by forty thousand NVA regulars, up by the DMZ. Alpha Battery fending off sappers who had penetrated their wire and commenced blowing up the compound in advance of a full frontal assault, and the temporary capture of Hue, where when the Marines finally battled their way back into the city and found what was described to me by an eye witness as: "The Asparagus Patch". Civilians who had been buried, dead or alive, in a park in the city with only their forearms poking up through the soil. In a ghastly apparition that lodged permanently in my mind as a field of nightmares and ghostly dreams. And it was not lost on me what a greater impact this must have had on the teller of the event, who had observed it firsthand.

It was on one of these **MEDCAP** missions to a village whose name I can't recall, somewhere in a straight line on the dirt road outside of Da Lai Pass, that I adopted Chesty. Named in honor of the famous Marine Corps hero: Chesty Puller. Chesty was the product of an odd and unexpected transaction with an old mamason with red beetle nut stained teeth, who made an offer to me that I couldn't refuse. It went just like this:

"Hey maween! You waunta buy a nice pump woasting puppy? Wun dawa."

What could I do? So I gave the apparently friendly old woman one dollar in exchange for the amazingly plump, light tan little puppy and quickly tucked him into the large hip pocket of my green camouflage utility shirt. Knowing if I had not done so that "Chesty" was soon to be summarily tenderized, executed, *woasted* and served on a bed of bamboo shoots, rice and peppers. Having earlier that day witnessed a tapeworm being coaxed and extracted, by virtue of the allure of a bowl of warm milk in front of the wide open mouth of a village child, I was in no mood for any more outrages and so Chesty was going back to base, but not as a take-out dinner.

Nothing seemed different that evening as I talked with Johnny, the new guy, by the lookout bunker. There were a few new guys who had just arrived earlier that day, and he and another guy had pulled perimeter watch and I was just acquainting myself with him as I had nothing else particular to do. I found myself impressed by his sincerity and somewhat jealous when he showed me a picture of his eighteen year old fiancée. He was from a southern state and had that peculiar charm, humor and intelligence that I had come to associate with that region. I remember especially coming away from that encounter with a mixture of fondness and envy. Fondness, because Johnny seemed like such a likable guy. Envy, because I didn't really have a girl back home that I could call my own.

That's the way I went to sleep that night, but I did have Chesty there in the hooch and I guess he was better than nothing. Anyway, it was TET, 1969 and there was a truce in effect and nobody seemed to think too much about it, but as it turned out, maybe we should have.

On February 23rd at, on, or about 02:30 hours, all hell broke loose. The way I remember it is like this. When the first explosion occurred, it was from within our compound. I popped up out of my cot and hurriedly put on my flak jacket. Other explosions were occurring simultaneously. The ground was shaking and flashes of light rebounding. The siren was wailing at a fevered pitch, but was being drowned out by the intense clamor of sound, explosions and small arms fire. By the time I exited my hooch, the whole compound was ablaze with internal demolitions and incoming rockets: 122 millimeter rockets, approximately seven feet long, were now raining down on our little hill with eighty souls, and the adjoining compound of HQ Company, First Battalion, Twenty Sixth Marines, of about another eighty souls.

Sappers, who had infiltrated the compound undetected, were underneath the hooches, shooting the occupants as they exited and throwing grenades into and under the hooches as they attempted to flee. As I came out of my hooch and turned to run up the hill to the trench where I was to form up the React Squad, I was stopped abruptly by Corporal Sarabella, soon to be Sergeant, whose duty it was to defend and ultimately destroy the heavy steel Conex container of secret documents with a 45 caliber pistol and a hand full of very large and ominous looking incendiary grenades, which, according to Corporal Sarabella, could melt steel!

So he shouts at me at the top of his lungs: "Stop!" And I do, two seconds before a mortar explodes in the exact spot I would have been if I had kept running. And he continues to shout: "The gooks have the top of the hill. They've got rifles and grenades. They killed the cooks!"

As I turn to go in another direction, away from the explosion of the mortar in front of me, another hooch takes a direct hit by a rocket. The rippled corrugated roof is thrown off of the exploding hooch high up into the black and fiery sky, quivering, reverberating and ultimately humming into an unbelievable, maniacal, hallucinogenic sort of scream. And then another and another direct hit. Now everything around me seems to be blowing into bits. The night black sky being torn and shattered and slapped by waves of concussion and blasting light.

43

Somehow, without thinking, I had managed to throw on my flak jacket, utility belt with loaded magazines, two bandoleers of extra ammo and my helmet. By the time I had burst through the front screen door of the hooch, I had jammed a magazine into my M16, cocked it and released the safety. I think I missed the wooden steps out the front of the hooch altogether and as I left Sarabella by the steel Conex box with his 45 in one hand and an incendiary grenade in the other, prepared to perform his final task and destroy the documents along with himself if necessary, in the last hopeless moments in the event of being totally overrun by the NVA battalion that was now apparently attempting to do just that, I did not feel nor would I feel, for some kind of time, the effects that running, jumping, falling, sliding and diving, would have on my bare feet.

The same bare feet that were taking me to the nearest part of the trench and the perimeter and would be taking me to places where I had never been before. Places that I would not want to return to. Places that I would never truly be able to leave:

"IT DON'T MEAN NOTHIN'"

"You can check out any time you like, but you can never leave."*

It's hard to remember things exactly. Some things I remember more than others. Mundane details are the first to go as if the more intense events absorb more of your brain and drown out the commonplace and routine occurrences.

And the most intense experiences, no matter how rapidly they transpire, always seem to be happening in slow tortured motion. Or even worse, reduced to a single live ever happening image. Not a snapshot, but an ongoing never changing event, like a part in a live scene from a play that never ends.

I know that I made it to the trench on the perimeter and joined the few others who were there in firing at phantoms out in the darkness, but with each flash of light from explosions and flares, the phantoms would disappear. They were not coming to this part of the perimeter so far as I could see and I was supposed to meet up on the

*(Hotel California, by the Eagles @ 1976)

hill and so, I began to make my way in that
direction. I left the trench and began making my
way up the hill. I came around and between some
burning hooches. Mortars and rockets were still
coming in. The sound is unbelievable.

Like a freight train coming down out of the
sky. With a runaway engine and its whistle being
ripped to shreds by a combustion too powerful to
be fully released.

Your night vision and hearing cannot quickly
recover from these assaults. But the next vision
that I was to behold would be one that would have
to be born permanently. As I came around one of
the hooches, one that was still standing, I
stopped. There laid out shoulder-to-shoulder on
the red ground before me, the red ground
illuminated in strobinar flashes of ungodly light,
six Marines on their backs, pressed against the
blood soaked soil, being administered to by the
corpsman who had just arrived that day from
Alpha Battery, on his way home on a thirty day
leave after being awarded a bronze star for
heroism in the field of fire, when Alpha was
almost overrun. All of the six Marines were alive

and all of them had bloody stumps where their feet were supposed to be. There was no sound.

My hearing may have been temporarily shut down by the deafening effect of the blasts, but I felt like the horrible intensity of the sight, the shock of reality, when I stopped and saw in shattered darkness and staccato flashes of light, that the blood in my body had broiled up to my head and expanded under pressure, pressing against the inside of my eardrums, leaving only blaring silence and the awful devastating sight.

Only for an instant and then I moved on.

I would later hear in a camp discussion an explanation of the traumatic lower leg amputations suffered by those six Marines, who had at the moment I encountered them, just then been dragged out of the burning ruins of a hooch that had received a direct hit by a rocket. An explanation that would always be difficult to accept, although it was provided by someone who had seen it happen before and was supported by the evidence witnessed by my own eyes. That when a rocket comes down through the roof in the center of a hooch, through the floor and explodes against the ground three or four feet below and

47

because the hooch is built on stilts against the incline of a hill, as most of ours were, that the force of the blast hurls the shrapnel of the disintegrated rocket upwards, in a circular pattern, in such a manner as to sever the feet or lower legs of the sleeping occupants arranged on their cots side-by-side, with their heads pointing outwards to the outside walls of the hooch.

Many things sound implausible unless you experience them first hand and even then they may be hard to reconcile. The experience of Corporal Flowers bears this out. Flowers had just recently transferred down from Okinawa where he had worked undercover for the Marine Corps Criminal Investigation Department. He was also very religious and would travel every Sunday from our base in Okinawa to the city of Naha, ostensibly for the purpose of gathering with other likeminded individuals for religious services but was, in truth, also meeting with his superiors for his undercover work. No one that I knew of was aware of his clandestine activities. I myself only became aware of it through my work as a Court Reporter shortly before I was transferred to Vietnam. This left me in somewhat of a quandary when Corporal Flowers arrived at Camp Henderson, assigned to the 1/13. Certainly no one in Camp Henderson, with the exception of maybe a couple of the most senior officers, knew of his background.

Now I liked Corporal Flowers and he was very religious, which was OK by me, even though my own religion was about to become KIA. Not my relationship with God mind you. Just the religious part. My relationship with God was to become one mostly characterized by intense anger, hatred, seething resentment and insufferable insignificance. All of it on my part of course. But a relationship none the less. But my main concern with Corporal Flowers was one for his own physical safety, as well as the well being of my fellow inhabitants of our little compound by Da Lai Pass.

Now I should probably explain something here that might come across as somewhat unconventional in the wisdom department, but it did, in my humble experience, become a sort of truism to me. You see, on rare occasion there were those who liked to indulge in a bit of cannabis now and then. A joint passed around during so called *down time* was not a common event, but not altogether unusual either. Booze was difficult to obtain and our two beers a day allotment was, for the most part, non-existent. There were no bars, restaurants, stores, or any other kind of commercial outlets in our immediate area and rarely did anyone get to a place where they were. However, for the price of a dollar, one could procure from a local village youth, for all the inherent risks involved of tampering, spiking, poisoning and getting busted, etc., etc., etc., what was referred to by its erstwhile adolescent marketeers, as a "party pack." Ten seven inch narrow, apparently machine rolled (like a Virginia Slim), marijuana cigarettes, reported to be 100% pure grown in Thailand weed.

Now I never saw anyone utilizing this illegal stimulant while on guard, on duty, or in any other capacity other than down time and one could certainly argue that an individual's readiness and combat effectiveness would be compromised as a result of its intoxicating effect. However, it is my own humble opinion, based upon the reality of shared experience, all other things being equal, that if I had to depend upon the reliability to function between someone who is drunk on liquor and one who is high on cannabis, in the event of the proverbial shit hitting the fan, I would expect more responsiveness from the latter. He might be more anxious, fearful and experience a greater intensity than normal, if that is even possible during the chaotic adrenaline rush of a combat event, but on the contrary, the drunk simply shuts down and becomes physically and mentally unable to function. I'll take fear over stupor any day. So long as you don't shut down.

Before I forget, as long as I am already out on the narrow end of a branch tottering from the tree of unconventional wisdom, allow me to make an assertion, perhaps based on firmer ground, on the subject of fear. I have read and heard over time, from those who profess to the ability of being fearless. Even and most disappointingly, from some who purported to be veterans with extensive combat experience.

Now of course, I can't speak for everybody, like everyone else, I am restricted by my own experience and limited faculties. Having acknowledged that however, I say without restraint - don't believe it! For the following reasons: The claimant is lying, for any of a variety of self serving purposes. The claimant was not involved in any truly horrific events. The claimant is not a veteran. The claimant is either a psychotic, schizophrenic, has absolutely no empathy for others, zero imagination or an IQ somewhere substantially below three digits. I make no pretense of courage, but if there is only one thing I learned over there, one thing I came away with, it is something wrought from the ages and it is this:

Courage is not the absence of fear. Courage is doing what needs to be done, in spite of the fear.

Anyway, so I told Corporal Flowers, soon to be Sergeant, that things were different in Vietnam. For one thing, everybody was armed. Some people for reasons you might expect were on shorter fuses. And how the only time I had been called upon to exercise any of my legal experience as a Court Reporter was when three military lawyers were summoned all the way from Okinawa to perform a preliminary investigation, for the purpose of finding cause, or not finding cause, to recommend Court Martial for a Marine who had been found in possession of a small amount of marijuana. This required a certain amount of the proper forms to be completed, interviews by the traveling lawyers with the essential people involved and their consequent findings and report. The upshot was a conversation and the remarks they made in my presence, immediately prior to their departure back to Danang and their return back home to Okinawa. They had a great time.

Three wonderful days and nights in the city of Danang, with all of its attendant perks and pleasures. Something that any of us would have required a hard to get in-country R&R to enjoy. They also appreciated the additional combat pay they were entitled to, simply by virtue of their mere presence *in country*, which was the term used to signify time spent in Vietnam. And they were most pleased with the potential affect that any time in I Corps, that is the northern most provinces of South Vietnam, properly annotated in their service record books, would have on the likelihood of future promotions. In fact, the form with their names, ranks, service numbers and dates of time in country, seemed to be of the utmost importance and the priority concern they had with me, during their very brief time spent at our camp, at the conclusion of their mission. Oh, and that the forms be properly authorized and duly signed by our commanding officer.

Other than that, since the Accused had not been found derelict in any official capacity, had an otherwise good record, was not involved in any wholesale trading of the illegal substance and due to the colossal time and expense of trying the Accused, punishment and the need to replace an already trained and transported *warm body*, the three traveling lawyers officially recommended against Court Martial, mused about how they could easily have come to this conclusion without the trip down *South* and concluded their visit with a burst of boisterous laughter, when one with his arms thrown up into the air for emphasis, beseeched his professional peers with an ere of feigned and indignant credulity and with the already shop-worn old cliché: "What are they going to do? Send him to Vietnam?"

Anyway, although I'm not especially proud to admit it, I presented sort of an ultimatum to Corporal Flowers. That considering as how it would be potentially dangerous for Flowers if word got out around camp about his background, it would be best if nobody was to find out and that if he was to cease and desist from his previous clandestine ways while he was a member of our unit, there would be no reason why anybody would have to know. As it turned out, this all became academic in short order, beginning with the very first moments that our camp was attacked. And it wasn't because he was killed. What happened is that Corporal Flowers was assigned that night to Corporal of the Guard and as such, was alone in a hooch that had radio contact via a land line to each of the guard posts, spaced out along the perimeter. In the event of any serious activity reported to him, or at the first sign of any incoming ordinance, he was to crank like hell and sound the alarm. Now nothing like this had happened since my arrival and not within recent memory from what I understood, and so rules and procedures were somewhat relaxed at that time for the Corporal of the Guard. Something that would change abruptly for everyone concerned from that point on.

In keeping with this lax state of affairs, the Corporal of the Guard, so long as he had the radio close by, was allowed to catch a bit of rest while on duty and the radio would make a loud squelch when it was activated, which was sure to wake him if he happened to be dozing. Consequently, Flowers was asleep on a cot when the assault began, but it wasn't the radio that roused him from his slumber. It was the explosion of three Chicom grenades thrown in rapid succession directly under the hooch beneath his cot. He came to on the ground three feet below where the floor used to be.

As he scrambled to get up from the ten foot wide hole in the floor, the door of the hooch flew open and the sapper, who had just thrown the grenades, burst in through the entrance way. At which point Flowers, who had somehow fortunately managed to locate his M16 at the edge of the unbroken portion of the floor, reached to pick it up. As he did so the sapper, unfortunately for Flowers, threw a satchel charge directly to the location where Flowers was reaching. And it exploded. Directly in front of him. Practically in his face. Flowers picks up the rifle, which fortunately had a magazine already inserted, cocks it, releases the safety and shoots the shit out of the sapper still standing in the doorway. Incredibly, he still manages to sound the siren. After all this, he has all of his parts still attached to his body in the places where they are supposed to be, he isn't blinded, no shrapnel sticking out at odd angles all over his body and no gashes, fractures, or gaping wounds.

By the time I saw him later that same day, when the sun had finally and surprisingly risen again in the sky, his whole conscious body was swollen like a ripe fruit from the concussions he had absorbed and every inch of his body was marked like a map of Tokyo with hair line blood tinged fissures where his skin was unable to stretch enough to accommodate the swelling. Corporal Flowers would never again sleep inside a hooch after that night and although he was able to carry out his duties, he would become more and more withdrawn, quiet and carried an expression as if he were in another place, some other time, or saw something that no one else could see. Everything happened in Vietnam.

But not everything is remembered and not everything is told. Lost with those who did not survive and with those who did not return. Lost in the chaos and confusion and the self protective suppression of the formidable and yet fragile mind. Sometimes that which affects you most is that which you can no longer see and is perhaps better left alone. But what of that which so stubbornly remains and cries out as it does from the darkness of time and says:

"I am here, I am still here, you will look at me, for I will never go away."

And so it was with the six Marines and their mangled legs, and the heroic Corpsman, who had only stopped for the night, as I quickly moved away into the broken and shattered darkness, for it was not my job to stay, but to move on, to join up with the others and take our positions on line at the heaviest point of impact, or at the breach. And as my hearing returned to a usable extent, I could hear and I could see the explosions and the rifle fire, AK47 chatter and M16's and grenades all within the compound itself and the incoming which continued to rain down upon us. When I finally rolled into the trench at the top of the hill, although very little clock time had actually elapsed, I was relieved to see the few other members of the React Squad who had just made their way up from the other side of the hill and to hear the first bit of good news. That the sappers who had taken the top of the hill and who had killed the cooks, were now dead. Killed only seconds before.

And so we made our way down from the trench to the perimeter where the quaking light revealed the blown bunkers of the lookout posts but no signs of life of the Marines who had manned them. I would later that morning find an unexploded Bangalore Torpedo inside the wire that had been either pushed or placed between the stilts of a hooch, directly under the cots of its sleeping occupants, that had somehow either not been detonated or had failed to detonate. But others had been detonated and had destroyed their targets, as well as by RPG's (Rocket Propelled Grenades) and hand thrown Chicom grenades.

The lookout bunkers at this point in the perimeter wire were gone. We took positions in individual fighting holes and the perimeter trench, to plug up the gap and opened up with our M16's to fill the field of fire to our front, but also looking to the sides and to the rear for infiltrators, mindful not to shoot one of our own. Sometime during that night, during a lull in the incoming, I heard my name being called out from behind. Back up on the hill. Most everyone was hunkered down and engaged in what had now become sporadic firefights with the phantoms outside the wire. I had no idea why I was wanted up there but I could tell by the tone of the summons that it was not a request. So I scrambled back up to where the sound of the voice had come from and was told to report to the captain who was hunkered down nearby. It was good news and bad news.

The good news was that a sapper had been discovered curled up under a hooch. The bad news was that the sapper was alive and curled up over six of the largest grenades I had ever seen in my life and that Sarabella and I had been *volunteered* to go under the hooch and capture him. Alive!

Now of course, I didn't like the sound of this and I wondered if we would even hear the sound of the explosion the six monstrous grenades would make if the sapper detonated just one. They would all explode. I don't know how Serabella got roped into it as he was supposed to be guarding his box, but as it turned out, Serabella took the worst part of it, although it was highly improbable that either one of us would survive if the sapper decided not to be captured. And it all came down to that decision. Sarabella gave someone his 45 and turned on a flashlight. I kept my M16 and under the hooch we went. We started crawling toward the sapper from opposing angles for just a little ways and then stopped each about 10 or 12 feet away. There hadn't really been too much time to think but what I saw under the hooch would definitely provide a shitload of food for thought later on.

I have never seen anyone shaking so hard as that sapper. In Minnesota it gets pretty cold and if you're not dressed for it and you stay out long enough, you can shake like a leaf. And I've seen people shaking from hypothermia, but none of it touches the shape and the shaking this sapper exhibited. My first impression was that along with the panic and sheer terror, that the sapper was under the influence of a strong drug and perhaps was in a state of withdrawal from the drug. Later that day or the next day, when inspecting the bodies of other dead sappers within our compound, someone pointed out to me a small pocket attached to the webbed belt on one of them and told me that the pocket was used to carry a vial of adrenaline. A potent stimulant. And that they would inject the adrenaline immediately prior to infiltrating the perimeter.

And so there we were under the hooch with Serabella, unarmed, shining the flashlight on the sapper. The sapper, wearing only faded green boxer shorts, was shaking spasmodically, actually vibrating, as if he was to shake with just a little more velocity, might actually disappear. Be beamed-up. Or whisked away to some other place. Except for the fact that he was tethered, by virtue of clutching with both of his hands a nest of grenades in a shallow depression before him. Like a delirious brooding mother hen guarding her precious eggs. Or perhaps he just couldn't let go.

And I was laid out in a prone firing position with a full magazine, my M16 set on full automatic aimed directly at his quivering head, desperately wondering which would it be. Would he submit to the repeated pleading by Serabella and accept "Chieu Hoi"? The program that sought to entice the NVA and Viet Cong to voluntarily surrender and roughly translated meant: "Open Arms"? Knowing what he and his comrades had just done? The full extent of which was not yet known and would not be known until daylight? Would I depress my own quivering finger, with just the slightest bit of additional pressure on the trigger of my rifle, releasing a stream of eighteen rounds of molten lead and turn his head into soup? Or would he pull the pin and blow us all to kingdom come?

How close can one be to pulling the trigger and not actually fire, with the flickering luminescence of the flashlight, the sapper's hands hidden and then revealed, in the inconstant blackness and light? Appearing to move but not moving, as Serabella slowly inches his way forward. The unsteady beam carving out a severe and shifting scene in the otherwise black and crowded space beneath the hooch.

"Chieu hoi, chieu hoi!" Whatever else Sarabella was saying, that's all that I could recognize. That and the ocean sound of blood pumping through my heart and rushing around my pulsing brain. But I didn't pull the trigger and the sapper didn't pull the pin and Serabella finally and simply took hold of the shaking sapper and pulled him away from the cluster of grenades. Away from the unthinking tools of our destruction. But the decision on the part of the sapper was, in the end, only of benefit to Serabella and me, for the sapper would not be alive when the sun passed over our heads the following day.

Yet it would seem like eternity before the first light of dawn. Serabella returned to his box and I to my hole. In the Marine Corps, they weren't called fox holes. They were called: "fighting holes". Our drill instructors were very clear about that. You got the impression that you weren't in a hole so that you could fox around but so that you could fight. Anyway, the prisoner was whisked away and we returned to what we were doing before and that was that.

Nothing much was said about it that I can recall. Things just happened. And as each moment of dragging darkness passed, punctuated by the breath-stopping shock of intermittent incoming and sporadic spasms of contagious volleys of rifle fire and especially as the surreal light of the most recent flickering flare sputtered and expired into the void, we braced ourselves for what seemed at each moment the inevitable culmination of the pattern and type of attack we had already endured: The penetration of the compound by an estimated three dozen highly skilled and fanatically motivated sappers, the barrage of devastating and disorientating aerial ordinance, the obliteration of fortified guard bunkers, the breach of the perimeter and, finally, the expected and dreaded full frontal human wave assault by a seasoned battalion of North Vietnamese regulars. Eager to avenge their fallen comrades who over the years had been devastated by the most feared and hated of American military ground weapons - *the artillery battalion* - and to do so by overrunning and utterly annihilating the occupants and communication nerve center of one such battalion. The relatively lightly armed Headquarters Battery of the First Battalion, Thirteenth Marines.

As the first faint glow of pre-dawn light began to subtly encroach upon the dark domain of night, before the actual rays of the sun had broken the crest of the jagged ridge of mountains to our east, the anxious anticipation of what seemed so inevitable began to gradually dissolve. But my moment of unrequited reverie was short lived and then, suddenly, shattered by the jolt of an unexpected command coming from above and behind me on the hill:

"Thompson, check out the area."

RED LIGHT

The light was barely perceptible as I scrambled out of the hole and as the blood rushed to regain its proper circulation in my suddenly unscrunched legs, the crimson light of dawn seeped into the hidden landscape of what had such a short time before been so familiar, but which now, with each tentative step appeared alien and uncertain. As if walking on the crust of unsupported ground. The whole world seemed to have stopped. I heard no one. I walked close to the incline of the hill, upwards and then to the left. Slowly. Without sound. My bare feet compelled me one foot before the other into an area that had remained hidden and unseen throughout the dark and explosive night.

The moon must have been covered, if it was out at all, and the glow from the as yet unseen sun, although gradually increasing, revealed the world around me but only as a cast of dark and shadowy shapes. Just as my feet appeared to me even at such close proximity, as they crept along the second ring from the bull's eye of a ten ring target which is what our hill had become. And in an area where wild grass had heroically yet sparsely managed to survive, my eyes strained to focus, at first glance, upon a peculiar dark shape that appeared out of place resting before me on the ground.

The dark shape drew me down and as I bent my legs to a crouched position to identify the object lying there on the ground before me, it seemed as if the pre-dawn light had intensified ever so slightly. There before me as my eyes flexed to focus on the object for as much detail as the slender light would allow, lay a large mat of what appeared to be hair. Human hair. And my mind went through a whirl of: "What the hell is that? It's hair! Where did it come from? How could it be? Why would somebody scalp someone?"

I didn't know what else to think. I was nineteen and I had never been in a real battle before and my brain actually translated what I was seeing from images instilled in my mind from old Western Movies seen as a child, where the Indians would during warfare, skin the scalps off their victims. As a trophy and as a warning to their enemy. As an act of terror. And as I took the scalp into my free hand these were the confused thoughts that were sailing through my brain, until I turned it over and I saw the ants.

I let it fall from my grasp. The light continued to increase. A few stuttering steps forward and I once again came to a halt and this time there was no ambiguity. It was a helmet. A helmet lying top side up on the ground as if someone had simply set it down, except that the whole back of it was missing. As if it had been neatly cut away with a hacksaw in a perfectly circular pattern. I lifted it with my free hand and slowly rotated it and there on the inside evenly spread throughout the interior of the helmet was a thick coating of what I immediately recognized as brains. And it was not until that moment that the mat of hair I had held in my hand only seconds before made sense. And as I dropped the helmet, stood up and looked to my left down the hill, I could see two utterly motionless standing stooped over shadowy figures, frozen in place, over the lifeless and headless body of "Tater". A silent silhouette of black against gray tinged with the color of rust of two unrecognizable fellow Marines hovering like mute sentries over the even less recognizable body before them. And the only thing that I knew for sure as I released the helmet and glanced to the left down the hill, is that whoever was lying there on the red ground had taken a direct hit by a hand thrown grenade to the back of the head. And the grenade had exploded at the precise moment that it made contact with the back of the helmet. And that this extraordinary coincidence of timing had resulted in blowing off and to bits the head of the Marine who had been wearing that helmet. The helmet I had been holding in my hand.

Only later would I learn that the helmet, the scalp and the headless body lying there in the early morning gloom at the feet of the two frozen faceless sentries belonged to Tater. One of our cooks. And the funniest guy in our outfit.

No, I didn't know that at the time. And though I didn't know him well, later I would see him clearly in all his splendor. A thin, wiry kind of guy from a southern state with pronounced even hawk like boney facial features and a rye mischievous expression. Always in the midst of a joke. Pulling at the arm or whispering into someone's ear.

The kind of guy who would immediately fall under suspicion when the only time we were treated to a feast of spaghetti and some kind of meatballs cooked up in two large steel vats and between scarfing forkfuls of the rare and precious stuff into my own overtaxed mouth, I just happened to glance to my right and see that the meatball properly impaled on the extended fork of the enthusiastic diner on the bench beside me had legs. Thin barbed insectual legs, dripping with the essence of finely crafted pasta sauce, from one of the unacceptably large mouse size cockroaches that were only too commonly heard and seen chirping and scurrying into their ground dug holes throughout our compound. And I, perhaps

71

not possessed of such a sophisticated sense of humor as the accomplished and dedicated culinary comedian who stood expectant, ladle-in-hand behind the steaming vat, did what I still deeply regret to this very day. I shouted: "Stop!" Never to know, to experience the exquisite sound and the culmination of Tater's random yet well played plan, of the actual *crunch* as the unsuspecting diner eagerly bored down with his determined teeth on the marinated exoskeleton of the giant cockroach meatball. No, it was not to be. But the idea and the image of Tater would always remain. Magnified in my mind as I am sure it was for the two silent witnesses who were also there and who are still there, who saw and still see.

It is this same specter that I still see and have always seen since it occurred. Not so much recalled, but seen as if it is still happening, perpetually, unending. The weird light. The eerie silence. The smells of acrid cordite and exposed flesh. The lingering smoke of burned and burning hooches and debris. The ghostly figures, shocked, motionless, transformed forever by the unacceptable and inscrutable sight lying mangled on the ground before them. Entering their eyes, their senses, their minds and their souls. The same slow and wary steps repeating on an extended and nightmarish treadmill where the levels instead of signifying an achieved goal, represent the unwanted but inescapable range of a growing and forced awareness.

From the shock and confusion of the large and intact mat of hair. The bloody ant covered hide on the underside of the scalp. Then a few more steps and the brain filled helmet with the back blown away in a semicircular pattern. Another step, as the dreadful realization sinks in. A glance to the left. Gazing on the confirmation of the dark and headless figure. Sprawled out against the cold morning ground.

And then a few more steps. I turn to the left a couple more paces to the east side of a large fighting hole which up until that moment, because of its shape and its depth, had remained no more than a black bowl of shadow in the periphery of my forward yet still darkened vision. And just as I come to a stop, turn and look down into the hole, the sun which had until that time been slowly ascending over the South China Sea, suddenly breaks the crest of the mountains to our east creating an effect like the flip of a switch on a powerful balcony spotlight focused upon the primary scene on a previously darkened stage.

And this is how I will always remember it. Something happened as the red light reflected off the ground and the interior of the hole and off the utterly still and lifeless bodies of the three Marines, seemingly posed close together, collapsed with the weight of the dead in the now starkly illuminated depression below me. Although all was still and all was quiet, it felt like a bitterly cold and damaging wind was blowing right through me. Through the very pores and cells of my motionless upright body. Blowing with a roar through my skull and my thoughtless brain. Coming from all directions at once but emanating especially from the frozen and wide open eyes of the one in the center. The one sitting upright against the far side of the hole facing and apparently staring, straight into me.

It was Johnny the New Guy. And the first thoughts that I thought when I was able to think were: "What about his eighteen year old fiancée? What about her?" And: "What about their parents who are planning the wedding?" And: "Why is it him instead of me?". Just like that. Boom boom boom.

But then as I turned and as I walked away and for the rest of my life, I wondered: "Where are their rifles, their helmets, their flak jackets?" How did Johnny end up in this hole when I had left him and I had last seen and spoken with him at the bunker, below, at the perimeter? Was he asleep in the trench outside of the bunker while his partner took his time on watch? Was he *boot kicked* out of slumber in the dead of night into a conscious nightmare by the sudden and utterly unexpected explosion of the rocket propelled or hand thrown grenade that destroyed the bunker and the occupant within it only a few feet away? Did he scramble from the trench in the chaos and confusion unable to locate his weapon, desperately clawing his way out of the trench and up the hill to the safety of the hole and the two other Marines, also new guys and also without weapons, only to be followed by and pursued by an insurgent NVA sapper who, when reaching the hole and standing at the same position where I had stood, looked down, depressed the trigger on his AK47 Assault Rifle and unleashed a volley of deadly lead into Johnny and the two other young Marines crouched up and pressed in on either side of him? Was this the last thing seen by Johnny's still open eyes? His final moment?

They looked like bullet holes to me. Even the first time and there wasn't very much blood. But there were at least four or five holes in Johnny in his chest, stomach, ribs and they had a bad color around the edges. Creating a flashing impression that the holes might just as well have been made by a red hot steel poker about the diameter of an average size index finger. But the rest of him was clean. No wounds on his face or his arms which were hanging limply at his sides. Palms and fingers partially opened. And the expression on his face. Mouth slightly open. His eyes! Almost as if...? As if he was waiting. Waiting for me to say something or do something. Like he had just asked a question or said something and was waiting for a response.

As if...?

But they were dead. Very dead. And their color was dead.

Dead.

In the red light.

DAYLIGHT

A lot of things happened during the night. Actually the early morning hours. The dark hours when people get sleepy, bored or inattentive. Or maybe thinking about things far away. Back in the World. A lot of things happened that I didn't see. Things that were hidden. Things that I can't remember or that I don't want to remember. Things happen fast. But they happen to people one at a time. Each person has his own world and it's the only world you've got. Individually. And when that world goes out it all goes out. Your world and all the other worlds. And whether it's just one world or a million worlds if yours is one of them for you it's the same thing. You're gone. Completely.

Poof!

These thoughts or something like them were what I was thinking as I carried the six service record books from the admin hooch to the medivac bunker. And I'm not sure when I did it. The record books in one hand, my rifle in the other.

The service record books of the six Marines from 1/13 who had been killed that night. With one final annotation in their records of service signifying the end of their tour of duty in Vietnam and their enlistment with the United States Marine Corps: "KIA". *Killed in action.* There were five more KIA from Headquarters Company, 26th Marines and one from the 1st Motor Battalion. Twelve KIA altogether from a total of about one hundred and sixty five Marines. And in the large heavily sand bagged medivac bunker built into the ground where the two mounds of our compound came together, where I had been ordered to deliver the service record books, my eyes and nose adjusted to the dark and dank environment inside and to the roughly forty to fifty wounded Marines crammed together on the dirt floor, from one sandbag wall to the other. By this time the most seriously wounded had already been evacuated from the compound.

Still later that same early morning, I would hear first hand from a returning patrol that had humped up to the ridge and who had subsequently discovered what was left of a seven man Observation Post that had been overrun during the night. The lead man in the patrol had a bad look on him, as perhaps we all did by this time, but there was something different about him and the other members of the patrol and I was there when they approached the wire and so I made a subtle inquiry, perhaps non-verbal and he said something just like this: "We found all seven of the guys on the OP. All seven of them are dead with their dicks cut off and stuck in their mouths."

That's what he said and then he just walked on by and I looked at each one of the faces of the patrol as they passed by and every one of them looked like an old broken man. These guys were with the 26th Marines, infantry and some of them had probably been around for some time. But I could tell that this event had scarred these guys forever. With an invisible wound more deeply and indelibly cut than what would qualify one to be awarded a Purple Heart. People say these kinds of things didn't happen, or they don't want to believe that they happened, but those people weren't there. And they weren't in that patrol, at that place, or at that time. Everything happened in Vietnam. And it happened to one person at a time.

Sometime that same morning, after leaving the medivac bunker and the returning patrol, I was walking up the hill towards the react trench heading for the S1 hooch and my own hooch on the other side of the hill. Perhaps to check up on Chesty who I had forgotten about up until that time. As I began to ascend, my neck and head cranked backwards as I heard once again, the now unmistakable sound of an incoming rocket and then, instantaneously, the blast and incendiary explosion as the rocket hit its mark on the other side of the hill. Immediately following its impact, another projectile descended and as I frantically scrambled up the hill for the relative safety of the trench, my head once again cocked backward and I saw and I heard the blazing, fiery, roaring ball of certain death coming in straight at me. Seemingly about to hit me square in the chest.

But it didn't. It struck and bounced no more than six to twelve inches from my right foot. The same foot, along with its close by partner, that somehow carried me and propelled me another twenty five feet or so to the trench. Which I collapsed into, still wondering how it was that I could actually be alive. It couldn't have been a rocket because it wasn't big enough. It must have been a mortar round that didn't explode. A dud. But mortars don't come in all aflame and roaring like a dragon as this one had. I just crouched alone in the trench and couldn't believe that I was alive and that my legs were still attached to my body.

But my eyes were peering over the lip of the trench. Back in the same direction I had just come from and where the *dud* had struck and bounced a mere pecker's length distance from my naked outstretched foot. My eyes were drawn to the broadside of a hooch directly below the point where the dud had ricocheted off the ground. There in the middle of the side of the hooch through the one inch thick wooden boards it was made of, was a six inch hole about half way up from the ground to the screen. Through the wall of the same hooch where just a handful of hours before Flowers had defeated the sapper, after climbing out of the ten foot hole in the floor, in an explosive face-to-face battle with no premonition or warning and had survived.

A couple of days later, when the opportunity presented itself, I would return to the hole in the hooch and the answer to the mystery of the unexploded dud would be revealed. It would take a couple of days to complete the revelation. First, I didn't make it over the hill as I initially set out to do that day or the next day for that matter. Instead, as sporadic incoming mortar rounds continued to fall, I found that I was unintentionally already in the right place. The react trench. I had sought the shelter of the trench simply because it was the closest hole I could find when the rocket and the dud came in. But soon I would realize that the other members of the react squad were already on position at the perimeter and had remained at their positions, as almost everyone else in our compound was on one-hundred-percent alert. So I sprang out of the trench during what appeared to be a lull in the incoming but as I darted for a hole by the perimeter, a mortar came in and it struck a short distance to the east of our hill and then something strange happened.

A slight breeze was blowing westerly and within moments of the impact of the last incoming round, the air was suddenly filled with a noxious and choking gas. Two or three things happened in quick succession. Somebody jumped up beside me and was choking like crazy. I looked down at the ruble of a blown out bunker and saw a gas mask lying there, partially buried in burst sandbags and I pulled it out and chucked it over to the choking Marine, who I also noticed did not have a weapon and as I did so, I grabbed a piece of cloth that did not appear to have blood on it and I stuffed it into my mouth. It actually seemed to work. A little. At least long enough for the breeze to eventually clear the gas away.

What the hell kind of gas it was I'll never know. It seemed really odd. Why would they lob a round or two of gas in on us? It didn't kill anyone and seemed to me to be similar in effect to the tear gas we were exposed to in boot camp. Where by squad we were led into a small bunker-like building with one door. After the door was sealed, the instructor, after explaining the proper way to use a gas mask, popped a tear gas canister flooding the room with the noxious substance. Then at a certain point he ordered us to remove our gas masks and immediately march in a circle right hand on the right shoulder of the marcher to your front. All the while choking out a miserable rendition of the Marine Corps Hymn.

You never heard such a pathetic, yet brave performance in your life. Unless of course you were there. A chorus of the insane! Especially towards the final verse. And when the instructor finally sprung the latch on our avenue of escape, after the final hallowed words of the sacred Hymn were sung, spluttered, or regurgitated from our frothing lips or *holes*; which is what our mouths were referred to during T.U.R.D, which stood for *Trainee Under Rigid Discipline*, we poured like a flushed toilet out into the open air with every orifice above our necks, except perhaps our ear holes, flowing like Niagara Falls. In an involuntary effort to purge our bodies of the violent vapors we were forced to ingest.

Anyway, as I plopped into an empty hole at the perimeter, I wondered if the mortar round had hit an ammo dump of our own. But there was nothing like that outside the compound. And to my knowledge, we didn't have any mortars anyway. And especially not any gas. The top of our weaponry consisted of one 50 caliber machine gun and two M60 machine guns. One online and the other M60 as a replacement. We had a few LAWs* and a couple M79 grenade launchers. Other than that, it was M16's, a few side arms, a shotgun, claymores and frags. The shotgun was carried by the point man on patrols. As a headquarters battery, we didn't have the firepower that the regular artillery batteries had. In other words we were vulnerable. And I won't even tell you how many NVA I was told were on the other side of the ridge. Outside of the Pass. It just

*(LAW - Light Anti-Tank Weapon)

wouldn't be believable. I used to think about the phonetic pronunciation of the name "Da Lai Pass". You know: *da lie*. But maybe that was just me. Anyway, I wasn't thinking about it when I jumped into the hole and pulled the rag out of my mouth.

But I was thinking of what had happened on the other side of the hill. And as soon as I could, I asked someone nearby if he knew what had happened. It wasn't just Chesty I was concerned about, but earlier that morning, when I had been checking out the area where I had come across Tater and Johnny, I had also encountered the corpsman with the Hispanic name, like Carlos or Juan, who had only stopped by for the night on his way to Danang and back to the World and a Bronze Star. But had instead spent the night treating amputees and wounded Marines of every description, under intense fire and chaos. When I came across him, he was utterly wasted. Used up. And so I practically ordered him to go to my hooch. To take my cot and go to sleep.

I have never admired anyone so much in my life as that selfless corpsman who I had only just met the day before. And I was never to see him again. The word I got, when I asked the guys nearby my hole, was that a 122 millimeter rocket had hit my hooch dead center. Completely destroying it. And I would never find even a trace of Chesty. And it was not lost on me the irony that Chesty, the *nice pump woasting puppy,* could not escape his fate. But I was not prepared for the miracle of the corpsman.

He wasn't killed! He was thrown out and through the hooch by the blast of the exploding rocket. He must have been, because the hooch, by the time I saw it, was burned to cinder. Both of his legs below his knees were described to me by the guys who loaded him onto the medivac chopper as: "dangling." By bits of flesh, muscle and tendon. The bones were completely broken. And because I myself cannot stand to think of this incident and how it took at least a week before we heard what had happened to the corpsman, thinking all the while that he most probably lost both of his legs, legs that had been dangling over my own cot, because of that, I will just say it right out. The doctors on the hospital ship outside of Danang, where he was taken by the medivac chopper, were incredible surgeons. Who were, we were told, at the forefront of their profession throughout the world. At the very cusp of new surgical skills and techniques. Of reattachment of limbs by piecing together the bones, stapling the torn tendons, suturing the ripped muscles and joining together the severed arteries and blood vessels with bits of plastic tubing. And that is what they did. They had a lot of practice. And they saved both of his legs. To us, it was a miracle. And the best news I ever got in Vietnam.

Hearing that news, I hardly noticed the practically naked bodies of the two dead NVA. One sprawled upon the other. They had been dumped not more than two feet from the side of the hole that I was crouching in. But I would notice them more throughout that night and the heat of the following day. And the cooling air of the next night as well. They would make themselves noticed. And indeed, I had noticed them earlier that same morning. Not long before. Being dragged in from outside the compound by ropes behind a jeep. I remember I didn't like the sight of it. I understood it. But I didn't like it. They had been killed or found dead by an early morning patrol out by the ridge. Anyway, they were to be my guests for the next forty-eight hours.

But first I would also hear what had become of the quivering sapper that Sarabella and I had captured under the hooch during the night. He had died of a "heart attack". For some strange reason this news disturbed me. It angered me. Even after everything that had happened, there was something about that shaking sapper that made me want him to live. After all, he hadn't pulled the pin. He could have easily killed us along with himself. And since he died anyway - you know. And I got the feeling that he never wanted to be where he was to begin with. And the communists had ways of making people do their bidding. And it wasn't very pretty. And the Intelligence guys that were brought in to question him and extract from him critical information, which may have been essential for ours and my own continued survival, didn't go under the hooch with Sarabella and myself.

They didn't face the dark specter of sudden death or dismemberment and look into the heartless eyes of oblivion. Only to survive, unscathed, because the one cornered and captured and under the influence of the most extreme pressure and fear, had decided to risk life over death.

Although I would have shot him in a heartbeat if he had made even the slightest threatening move and although I already hated the communist bastards with a passion because of what they were doing, I didn't hate *that* man. And I have never really been sure of what killed him. And I never before told anyone how I felt about it. I just wanted him to live.

Then something completely unexpected happened. We began to notice a huge black cloud approaching our location. You could see it billowing, ever larger, trailing back for miles in a southerly direction. The appearance of the monstrous black cloud had been preceded for some time by the ongoing sound of low rumbling explosions from the same direction to the south. The continuous sound of the explosions was muffled, as if coming from a good distance away, but you could still feel it through the ground and through the atmosphere and we had assumed that it must have been a B52 strike dropping hundreds of large, perhaps 500 pound bombs, on a wide swath of area like a big strip of carpet being gradually unrolled on the floor. The bombs going off in steady succession. But we were wrong. And as the impenetrable coal black cloud widened and enveloped us completely we received confirmation by radio that a huge ammo dump and stockpile of 250 and 500 pound bombs had been set off. The official explanation? A grass fire that had gotten away from a local farmer.

But we hadn't been born yesterday. And we figured for sure it had been set off by sappers or incoming. The ammo dump continued to cook off for the next three days and nights and although it was 10 to 15 miles away, as long as the wind continued in our direction, the massive column of black soot utterly blotted out the sky above us and the landscape around us. As a dense and persistent sheath of tiny particles of cinder fell like black sleet. With a sound like sand being sprinkled on a plate of smooth glass. It rained down upon our helmets. On the plastic stocks of our rifles. Which were pointed out into the gloom.

And as the last of the light succumbed to the eerie shroud that enveloped our world like the final Day of Judgment, we figured for sure that this could only portend like the omens of old the coming of the Lord. Or more appropriate to our situation, a large scale attack by our adversaries.

So we hunkered down and the black sleet fell like drizzle.

And not even a flare could pierce the darkness.

PAINT IT BLACK

*"I see a red door and I want it painted black. No colors anymore I want them to turn black."**

If that was my wish, it certainly came true.

A Twilight Zone like atmosphere took hold and it didn't let go for some time. Darkness had never been so tangible. You could feel it. Hear it and smell it. And you half expected ghosts to appear. To push their way through the gloom and the dead to walk. But what I recall most about that time and what lingers still, are the

*(Paint It Black, by the Rolling Stones @ 1966 ©)

94

gradually released sounds and smells emanating from the two rapidly decaying corpses intertwined in a sort of deathbed embrace a couple of feet from the edge of my hole. And the odd thing is, I never even considered moving them. The odor came first as the sweltering heat of the day took hold. All in unnatural darkness. And it grew as the hours passed and as their bodies swelled.

Yes, I could see them because during the day the blizzard of ash and cinder allowed an ever decreasing visual spectrum of approximately 10 to 20 feet. But from there on it was like looking into oblivion. The hours of utter silence crawled by, covered with the hiss of falling ash and as they did so, slowly and almost imperceptibly, the day gave over to night. And then the sounds began.

Sounds that mocked the long periods of silence between sporadic spasms of rifle fire and intermittent incoming rockets and mortars. Soft sounds. Close yet seemingly from another world.

Gurgling, hissing and whistling sounds, coming from the insides of my two steadfast intimate companions as their now enormously swollen and extended torsos began to cool and constrict.

Wheezing and spluttering from their mouths and rectums as they gradually deflated. During their rapid decomposition, gasses had built up inside of them and during the advancing heat of the day, had expanded. And as the air cooled somewhat throughout the night, they were expelled from the putrefying human balloons that seemed somehow impossibly to be almost alive. For two days and nights. And for fifteen years off and on, without warning or premonition, I would suddenly sense the taste and the odor of death and human decay. It rose up from within me seemingly from my lungs and I never told anybody about it.

For years I thought that my lungs were rotting, but every single time that it happened, that the unmistakable taste of rotting death would rise up in my throat, I would immediately think of those two dead NVA, intertwined in their macabre embrace and how over the time we spent together, *so close,* that I must have inhaled and absorbed billions of their departing molecules. And that those same rarefied molecules had stayed buried deep in my lungs. Stored there and expelled in part, over time, in a sporadic way until one day after fifteen years, it just stopped and never happened again. Of course I couldn't say anything. People would have thought that I was crazy.

And so the sun did not show its face again that day as the black cloud of cinder particles covered and filled the sky around us. Settling unnaturally on the ridge, the bush, the rice paddy and the red ground.

The dark of night moved in like black on black but still somehow we could feel it change. Like a dark blanket being lowered on you in an already darkened room. Everything seemed smaller.

Closer.

Yet Alverez, Johnson, Carter, Sarabella, they all seemed like they were a million miles away. It got dark. It got so dark that time itself seemed to change. And it did.

The next thing that I remember was not the next morning, but the following morning and I was out of my hole and up by the armor's shack. Not to get ammo or because of a weapon problem, but to see if I could get some clothes.

And most importantly, some boots. The armor kind of doubled up on supply items, so it was not an unusual request and I am sure that he didn't mean anything by it when he pointed to the pile of rumpled clothes on the ground in front of the shack.

He didn't have anything new in stock. So I reached down and pulled a utility shirt and trousers from the top of the pile. I held them up in the air to check them for size and there were holes and large holes clear through them. And wet and drying blood. Some parts completely saturated with a brown oily darkened color of red on green. And I just lost it. I threw them down like I was throwing a rock into the face of a flesh eating rat. And I cursed it without thought, without restraint and I later felt bad for the armor. But it was all that I could do to keep my trigger finger off of my rifle and to keep from exploding as I stomped away.

It was either then or a short time thereafter that I once again took sight on the hole in the hooch made by the *dud* that had come calling on me a couple of days before. I walked straight towards it. Bent down and peered through what was left of the floor inside. I went around to the door where the sapper had burst in and charged Corporal Flowers. Went into the hooch. Down into the hole blown out by the chicom grenades and there on the ground beneath the ruins of the blown out floor of the hooch lay the answer to the mystery that had sunk into my brain like a large rock into a small pool of water. Up in the trench where I had collapsed a couple of days before.

And I looked at it lying there for who knows how long, in the quiet of the desolate dust filled hooch as my mind filtered through the haze of recent events. Time had taken on a new quality. A new face. It seemed elongated and disjointed. It seemed as if it had been stretched out. Stacked up. Compressed. And imbued with an unnatural weight. But I somehow knew what I was looking at and where it had come from. When I finally reached down under the still raised but shattered boards of the floor and picked it up, I was immediately surprised at how heavy it was, compared to its size. It was round and about four or five inches across and at least two inches thick. With a hole in the middle. It was solid steel or some kind of heavy metal. With jagged edges and it looked like a gear, except that the sprockets around its circumference were broken off. And what were sheared off were the blades of the rear propulsion propeller of the rocket that had hit and destroyed my hooch on the other side of the hill.

The rocket that had practically severed the legs off the corpsman and blew Chesty to smithereens. And then, as if with intent, the rocket propeller was hurled over the hill. A spinning, roaring, ball of flame. Landing and ricocheting only inches from my right foot. I picked it up. And I kept it. I still have it to this day. Wrapped up in a black piece of cloth. Sitting in a dark drawer.

I didn't get any clothes that day and it was the next day or maybe the one after that and we were on a sweep patrol of the area on the north side of our compound between the wire and the ridge. I remember that the Captain from the 26th Marines who was in charge of the patrol had a unique weapon. It was a Thompson Sub Machine Gun. At least that is what I imagined it to be. It was 45 caliber and had a steel fold down stock that consisted of nothing more than a rod that came straight back from the barrel, looped down and back up, creating a brace for the shoulder. From

there back up to the barrel parallel on either side.
Kind of a loop that was bent down at the end. I
don't know why I remember that so well, when I
have forgotten so much else. It just seemed odd
or unique. It made me wonder where that
Captain had been and how and where he had
come by such a weapon. It looked like it was
homemade. I'm sure it wasn't a *Thompson*.
Even though that is my last name. Maybe it was a
Burp-Gun. Whatever, it was a nasty sucker. At
least at close range.

But it left me wondering about that Captain
from the 26th Marines. But then it seemed like
you were always left wondering about something.
Like why didn't Staff Sergeant Jackson get down?
On that very same patrol when somebody hollered
out: "Fire in the hole!" I wondered what he was
thinking about. We had discovered some spider
holes and perhaps tunnels on the outside of a
berm or rice paddy dike. The order had been
given to blow them and right before the grenades
went into the first one, the warning was called out
and everyone got down except Staff Sergeant
Jackson. He just remained standing there until
the shrapnel caught him in the face.

It seemed really odd to me. Because of what happened to the Staff Sergeants. There weren't many of them left. It became what is known as: "Lessons Learned". You see, most of the Staff Sergeants in 1/13 were together in one hooch. And that was one of the hooches that had taken a direct hit by a 122mm rocket. It was determined thereafter by Command never again to group up personnel by either rank or specialty. Otherwise you could lose them all in one incident. And I had to think that *that* had to be bearing down on Staff Sergeant Jackson's mind. How lucky he was that he wasn't in that hooch. The one that got blown to hell. But no, he just stood there. Until the shrapnel dropped him. But he lived and I am glad that he did. I really liked him.

He worked in the S1 hooch and he was kind of like my superior, as a senior non-commissioned officer. He was black and he had been in the Corps for a long time. But he didn't throw his weight around and he was a genuinely nice guy. And he looked like a wolf. He really did. Or maybe like a coyote. And he had this one other really peculiar characteristic. Actually it was a behavior. Out of his little green folding camouflage desk - a remarkably economical and efficient piece of portable military office furniture which collapsed into a rectangular chest, straps and typewriter included - he would pull a paperclip from a little cubbyhole drawer, unfold it so that one end of it was completely distended and insert the pointed end directly into his ear. Then, as he slowly twirled the extended tip of the unfolded paperclip deep into his inner ear, a most amazing continence would overtake the features of his wolfish face. A look of sheer bliss. He would exhibit a meditative or transcendental pose like the state of nirvana achieved by Tibetan monks in the fabled temples of Shangri La, on the steppes of the Himalayan Mountains.

You had to see it to believe it. And I was really glad that he lived, but of course after we medivaced him we never saw him again. And it occurred to me that maybe he didn't actually hear "fire in the hole" when it was clearly called out. And he was close by. Close to the hole. Maybe he was hearing some other kind of sound caused by the latent effects of the twirling paperclip. Maybe it was a constant buzz or maybe the chanting bells and horns of Shangri La but whatever it was, Staff

Sergeant Jackson didn't drop. He just stood there. And it makes you wonder. Or more so, it leaves you wondering.

But then something else happens that makes you wonder and so forth and so on and well, you get the picture. Before you know it, you've got a look on your own face somewhere in the range between Corporal Flower's and Sergeant Jackson's. Or worse. Like the guys in the patrol that came down from the ridge the morning after. Anyway, it makes you wonder. And makes you realize what wondering can do. So pretty soon you stop wondering, or at least you try to. Either way it changes your face.

But you never really stop wondering. And sometimes it seems like that is all that is left. You're standing over the lifeless, cold, staring eyes of Johnny the New Guy or you are staring into Tater's helmet. Or you're waiting alone in a hole in utter blackness engulfed in the suffocating stench of rotting death and you're wondering: "Where are they? Why didn't they finish the attack?" Finish us off when they had the element of complete surprise? Had we actually driven them off? Intelligence from the sapper POW had revealed the identity of the NVA battalion that had launched the assault. And they had inside information regarding our compound. One of the sappers we found dead in the perimeter wire was identified as one of the Vietnamese barbers that were allowed into the camp about once every month or so. The same barber who had cut my own hair and whose hand had wielded a straight edged razor trimming my meager sideburns and shaving the sparse whiskers on my face and neck. And whose hands had gently run warm scented water from a bowl over my reclining head. Massaging it into my scalp as a very pleasurable finishing touch upon completion of his deft handiwork

Of course later, I would have to wonder. What was he thinking when he was doing this? And what was he thinking during his last moments? Entangled in the razor sharp wire as his body received a barrage of burning bullets from our hurriedly assembled defensive rifle fire? Directly out from where I had first made it to the wire after scrambling from my hooch the first night. Was he forced to take part by intimidation and vile threats to members of his family? Or was he a true believer? Either way he had been the source of inside intelligence and had most probably stepped off precise measurements within our compound, providing the NVA battalion with exact coordinates to facilitate their aerial and ground assault. And for his efforts he was rewarded by being included in what he had to know was a suicidal operation. Especially if the approximately thirty five sappers who had stealthily infiltrated our compound were never intended to be backed up. By a full scale invasion. The attack from the inside coincided with the assault from the air. The rockets and mortars coming down and the RPG's being fired into the perimeter lookout bunkers seemed to be the signal for the sappers already inside to begin their demolitions. And they did. At least most of them. Of course the barber never made it inside. Again. Not since he had cut my hair and run the straight edge razor up and down my neck. He never even made it through the wire.

No, he was left like a torn and dangling scarecrow to greet our pensive eyes in the early morning mist of first light.

THE LISTENING POST

A few days after the incredible arrival of Captain Smiley but before the Seabees* came to build new replacement hooches and prior to beginning the monumental task of constructing the new three rings of razor studded spiraling concertina wire around the perimeter, the CO came up with a whole new concept of how to execute a proper method of military defensive strategy. At least for us it was new. And of course he was right. Gone were the rice farmers from the rice paddies outside of our compound. Gone was

*(Seabees *CBs* -- Naval Construction Battalion)

the little boy with his little stick and the massive longhorn water buffalo he perched upon as he gingerly yet languidly guided the mammoth creature through the iridescent sheen and sun flecked surface of the jade colored water garden. Through the flooded labyrinth of delicate rows of ripening rice.

Gone was the usual clutch of ancient old mamasons who vigorously chewed and spat their red or black beetle nut, like punctuation points, during momentary pauses in their singsong revelry. The pitch and volume of their animated discussions would rise and fall and rise again to seemingly untenable levels of shrieking and wailing, yet with a distinctive musical quality, even though you felt certain that at any moment they would surely come to blows.

The urgency and passion engendered in the expression of their increasingly archaic dialect seemed to always be heading to an imminent collapse, plummeting into unbridled violence. But it never really did. For all I knew, the feisty old mamasons could have simply been ruminating over the proper preparation of their favorite recipes. And it seemed like they had been there unchanged, spitting and quarreling for a thousand years. But all at once they were gone. And they never came back. And the CO had a new plan and it was a good one. We all had a new way of looking at things. A new perspective. And I don't remember ever hearing the word *volunteer* mentioned. But three guys would be going out on our first Listening Post. Three guys would be stationed about five or six hundred meters outside of the wire where they would spend the night. Alone. Listening.

Without a radio. And because of the distance and the terrain involved, realistically, without any backup. And it would be dark. Which would serve as both an advantage and a disadvantage. Depending upon the circumstances. All of which and more was playing around in the fevered brains in various unspoken ways of Johnson, Alverez and myself. Two PFCs and a lance corporal. And because as the lance corporal I held the senior rank, I was designated to be in charge. Which meant that I would carry the green flare. The green flare was a signal to the Marines inside the wire that *friendlies* were coming in and was to be used in the event that the LP, for whatever reasons, had to return to the compound. Especially during the dark of night. And that they would prefer not to be shot as they approached the perimeter. But generally, it was only to be used for emergencies. However, for us at that time, there really was no *generally* as none of the three of us had ever been on an LP before.

So I hoped that we wouldn't have to use it. Still, although it didn't seem like much in the way of insurance, I fastened it securely to my flak jacket, as we did the grenades and perhaps too much ammunition. If that is even possible. And we taped or excluded everything that could jiggle or make any noise whatsoever. We applied camouflage paint to our faces and hands to mute the glow and reflectiveness of our alien skins. Just like real grunts. That is unless you could see, smell, or taste the retched insecurity and unadmitable fear boiling up in the shameful and lonely pools of privacy behind our flickering eyes.

Really, nothing was supposed to happen. It was a big area out there. And there would be only the three of us. Our assignment was to hunker down close together so that we could use hand signals if need be and to be as quiet as possible. To simply listen. What were the chances that the enemy, even if they did decide to probe the area, would come anywhere even close to our position?

But as the twelve man patrol slowly snaked its way in the late afternoon sun to the patchy bush covered area on the far side of the open rice paddies, which was to be our drop off point, a couple of unsettling thoughts seemed to have ascended to the surface of my by now, roiling consciousness. And they would stubbornly remain there. One of them was this: If twelve men went into the bush covered area, which wasn't that large of a patch to begin with and only nine men came out of the other side, since there was still sufficient light for any eyes to see from any one of about a billion concealed locations on the nearby slopes of the mountainous ridge, wouldn't it be incredibly obvious what happened? Even for the most mathematically challenged gook in the whole wide world?

Yeah, we called them gooks. Ironically, I had heard that the word actually meant *foreigner*. Don't really know if it does, but you couldn't go around everyday using multi-syllable words for everything could you? Anyway, the other thought was this: If we did hear or, God forbid, see any movement out there, how in the hell were we supposed to tell anybody about it? The issue of the radio was discussed and dismissed in about five seconds. It was too far out to run a wire. That was the explanation. Also, there were large areas of rice paddy between the LP location and the perimeter. And of course it occurred to me that you couldn't use a radio that made any noise. A sharp *squelch* surrounded by hours of silent darkness and you might as well turn on the "Hit Parade".

We didn't have any of the more sophisticated remote phones like the big boys used. In fact, I don't think I had ever even seen one. We hadn't seen the Movies yet. And so, with great subtlety and absolutely no fanfare, we sank into the bush as the other nine members of the patrol continued through and out the other side. Without even breaking stride. Everything was hunky dory for about two seconds. Then the first glitch occurred. We had settled down into a close-knit triangular formation no more than three or four feet apart. Unfortunately for myself, I had settled down into a large, still fresh, pool of blood. Human blood. Left there by at least one NVA attacker that we wouldn't have to be listening for. His body dragged away previously either by them or by us.

I adjusted slightly so as not to be directly in the pool of blood, but not by much. The concealment that we had was not extensive and we wanted to be in the middle of it. We took our positions and we wouldn't move from them until such time that we would evacuate the LP. In fact we wouldn't move at all. But the sun moved, or the world turned and it did so rapidly and by the time the rest of the patrol was nearing the gate in the perimeter wire, the great solar globe had softly sunk behind the jagged crest of the western mountains. Like a mournful kiss good-bye.

Then the long hours began. The only words were those that formed silently upon the blackboards within our minds. Forming, fading and forming again. By midnight or zero hour, we had already been there for over six hours. Your senses become unbelievably intense. Practically unbearable. You hear everything. Even the pulsing of your own blood.

There were always wild animals around. We saw them routinely. Small wild cats, deer mouse, or is it deer mice? Those kinds of things. And you could smell the blood. That is if you let yourself think about it. But the one thing I hadn't thought about was a four letter word that had already formed on my mental blackboard along with a whole string of other four letter words, which was now blinking and blazing like a hot bright red neon billboard sign that read:

ANTS!!!

They had smelled the blood. And now and for hours to come the ants were exploring every available orifice that my body provided for them. Especially my face. Ears, eyes, nostrils and mouth. Which was the only thing I could really keep closed. But I didn't touch them and I didn't move. And sometimes the sweat would wash one down a little ways and he would begin his ascent all over again. But they didn't bite me. And I figured that they were drawn to the blood pool and then to the blood that had gotten on my boots and pants. From there they followed up the contours of my crouching body to the highest ground and the most exposed surface searching for the wound and the source of the spilled blood. But try as hard and as persistently as they did, they didn't find it. But each one had to find out for himself. I guess they didn't have a radio either.

And so it went. The minutes continued to crawl by like the tiny feet of the ants and I could feel every one of them. And I could hear everything and although it was very dark, I could see just slightly but enough to make out the motionless crouched shapes of Johnson and Alvarez, just three to four feet away. And I wondered what was going on inside their heads. Under the helmet.

I really didn't know them all that well. I remember feeling a bit uncomfortable and perhaps embarrassed when I observed Johnson clicking away with his Instamatic camera, pictures of the dead and mangled bodies of the sappers around our compound. Besides rifle fire, there were a lot of grenades thrown around. There was even a report of some hand-to-hand fighting, although I didn't see it myself. But then there was a lot that I didn't see. Some of the bodies were pretty messed up and I wondered why did he want pictures of them? And who in the hell would he show them to and why weren't the pictures in his brain enough? But he wasn't taking pictures of any of our own guys and it was none of my business anyway, so I kept my mouth shut. But I wondered.

Alvarez on the other hand was one of the most optimistic guys I ever met. He was of Cuban descent. In fact, he was from Cuba. Having immigrated to America with his family as a young boy. And he was proud to be an American and proud to be a fighting man for his new Country and, of course, proud to be a Marine.

Then the other sounds began. Somewhere around the bewitching hour. About 02:30 hours. Which is about halfway through the second watch. Long enough after the first watch had eagerly nestled into their *rubber ladies.* The Marine green air mattresses they had dragged down to the perimeter trench and had fallen quickly and soundly into careless sleep, for the second watch to have stared into the black nothingness before them and to have fallen into the realm of the wake dreams. Waking dreams. Tired blinking heavy syrupy dreams. When your

116

eyelids stick together and you can actually hear a noise when you force them apart. And also enough time before sunrise for the enemy to execute an objective and retreat under cover of darkness. But the six dilated eyes of the long time listening LP weren't blinking. And the sounds we were hearing were a long way from the wake-dreaming nodders back behind the wire.

Have you ever been alone in the woods, being real quiet and just listen? It's amazing how much noise a small animal can make. A squirrel or a bird just jumping around gives the impression of something much larger. A deer or a bear has a steadier cadence. Makes less noise when it walks but produces a greater gravity with the sound of each step. Cats hardly make any noise at all. But no matter what kind of animal, wild animal, that you might hear prowling about, there is one sound that you will not hear it make. And after all the dark hours and all the dark sounds and long after our physical bodies had seemed to not even exist, having succumbed to the dominant primeval power of the utterly seductive nocturnal environment around us and had dispersed into the soupy and quivering atmosphere like bodiless particles of sensory energy, my ears, which seemed to have expanded to proportions that would make even the largest of bull elephants proud to possess, picked up a tiny sound. A tiny sound that roared its way back into my breathless consciousness like a zillion volts of heart-stopping electricity. As if a frigid hand had been thrust into my sweating ant covered chest and had coldly and heartlessly crushed the mortal muscle which had been beating only a moment before:

"Clink...."

That's all it was. But with that one little sound every part of my extended being came rushing back to its center with the force and the gravity of a cosmic black hole. It was the sound of something metal. And it was not far away. About ten to twenty meters directly forward of our position. And it could only be one thing. Human. There it was again. Another *clink*. And then another and the sound of the bush being moved and then footsteps softly breaking through the underbrush.

They had to be coming directly toward our position! Of all the area to the left and to the right of us, they just had to be coming right smack dab, straight as an arrow, directly toward our exact location. Almost as if they too had smelled the blood. Or like they knew we were there. And it didn't take long, but then time had already completely disappeared, as well as everything else in the entire world. Except the sounds of the brush breaking. The muted sounds of footsteps coming ever closer and the clinking sounds of something manmade:

"Clink, clank, clonk, clunk."

Not loud, but distinct. Something like the metal swivel hinge on the webbed sling of an AK47 Assault Rifle. Swinging from the motion of being carried and hitting occasionally against the stock of the weapon it was attached to. Or something dangling from a utility belt like a grenade and a steel ammo cartridge making contact. But whatever it was, it was like a mouse that roared and for us it could only mean one thing. We were screwed. That is. Unless we did everything right. The first time, because we weren't going to get a second chance. Our listening mission was going to have to change and it would do so abruptly.

I don't remember that there were any other options going through my head. There really wasn't any time to think. Perhaps someone else would have done things differently. I don't know. They just kept coming right at us and the sounds got louder and closer and it sounded like there was a bunch of them. If we didn't do something soon they were going to be right on top of us, in just a few seconds. And they were.

But during those few seconds, which had elapsed between the sound of the first *clink* and the moment the raised foot and lower leg of the point man of the NVA patrol parted the branches of the bush, directly into our position, some two to three feet from my face, I had already slowly and quietly reached over to Johnson, who likewise reached over and put his hand on Alverez. And with both of them straining to see my hands, I went through the mock motions of pulling the pin from a hand grenade and then held up two fingers, as if flashing them the peace sign, which was fashionable during those times in another world. I followed that with a two handed lobbing motion and then I pointed to the east, in the same direction that we had come from when we had taken our position, some nine or ten hours earlier. And I gave the point sign a couple of poking motions for emphasis. Oh, and I quietly slipped out the green flare and held it up close to my face to determine for sure which end was the detonator end and I gently laid it down along side of my rifle, pointed in the same direction.

Now it's easy to get all worked up about why things happen the way they do and how people act and react to the circumstances they find themselves in. And I have thought about it many times and of all the questions that have come to mind, I have never once asked myself: "What would John Wayne have done?" It wasn't like that. It wasn't like a movie. It was like a dream. A very bad dream. Except that you are wide awake and you can't stop it...

Now!! It was a silent scream. We hurled the grenades. All six of them. The bush immediately in front of us was moving. Parting. And that is when we lobbed the grenades up into the air. All in the direction of the by now distinct and unmistakable sounds of the oncoming patrol. And before any of the grenades had even hit the ground and as the foot and the lower leg were breaking through the bush, I had jammed the butt end of the green flare against the ground:

"Swooshhh!"

And as one we opened up firing our M16's on full automatic as we moved out quick but low, in a file. Johnson, then Alverez and myself in the rear. We moved at a right angle from the point of the encroaching patrol firing nonstop into the black and evil menace that didn't just kill, but had mutilated and debased our dead and wounded brothers. The barrels of our rifles remained on target like swiveling turrets as we moved. As *if they knew what to do*. And as the grenades exploded in double staccato blasts, three times in rapid succession, the green flare popped off in the black and airy sea high above casting a pale and eerie light on the malevolent and tumultuous ground below. We ripped the empty magazines from our weapons, jammed in fresh replacements and we gained the element of pervasive and dominant firepower, interrupted only momentarily by the timing of the grenades.

We made it to a spot some twenty or so meters away flanking the line of the enemy patrol, stopped and hit the deck, but we never stopped firing except to reload. And we immediately began a maneuver that seemed to just happen. As if out of thin air. Well not exactly. Because when we reached the position outside of the clump of bush we had just exploded and fired our way out of, something else began to fill the air. And it wasn't just the pale green luminescence of the flickering flare or the returning fire of the surprised and besieged enemy patrol. It was coming from behind us. From our own compound.

The sudden roar of rifle and machine-gun fire filled the chaotic atmosphere, electrifying the hostile ground we clung to, as the perimeter defenders of our sanctuary opened up with everything that they had. Including M79 Grenade Launchers, whose offspring were now descending and exploding at the limit of their range close to our position. They were firing at us. At us! It didn't make any sense. Unless? We had to do something. We truly were *in the middle of it*.

I don't know how it happened or remember what was said. It was like we were on automatic. While Alverez and I kept up a steady stream of fire, Johnson pulled back about twenty meters in the direction of the perimeter, reloading on the run. When he got to his position he dropped to a crouch and opened up. As soon as I needed to reload I took off towards Johnson, reloading on the run. This all happened in a very short period of time. Some kind of time. When I got to Johnson's position I immediately opened up as Johnson reloaded and then finally, Alverez pulled out but about halfway to our position he did something unexpected.

He stopped. He stopped and standing straight up in the air, he turned and commenced firing nonstop, oblivious to everything except the ravaged bush and the focus of his rage within it. Alverez didn't want to leave. He was a man possessed. As if on cue and in order to highlight the unfolding spectacle, it just *had* to happen. Even with the cacophony of exploding sounds breaking about us, you could hear it coming and then: "pop". Directly above us, the *white illumination flare* ignited and lit us up like the Miesville Mudhens: playing baseball on a Saturday night.

Except that instead of cheering us, or even booing us, all the spectators were armed to the teeth and hell-bent on killing us.

It was just too much. With everything that had happened, the way things turned out, we really didn't need the flare. But that is exactly what happened. They lit us up. And with Alverez firing away like a crazy man, standing straight up out in the open for all the world to see, directly in my line of fire, I stood up. And they hadn't stopped firing at us from behind, but no matter how much I hollered at Alverez to fall back, he wasn't about to stop.

It was like somebody had flipped his switch and he was stuck on *maniac*. So I joined him. In the bright light and in order to get a better angle, I stood up and commenced firing on full automatic, no more than a couple of feet to the left of Alverez's head and shoulder and I was still yelling at him to pull back. The whole idea of the constant fire was to not give the enemy a chance to recover or to respond. But we didn't know if there were others out there or which direction they would come at us from and it seemed like the bullets were coming at us from all directions.

It was...words cannot describe it. Standing out there. The roar around us. And the roar within. Like it was raining but we weren't getting wet. Standing out there in the falling light of the flare. Utterly exposed to the hail of hot lead zipping and cracking in the static air. Ripping through the grass and brush around us as the M79 grenades burst into showers of white light and sprays of sparks like haphazard lightning strikes.

And it was some kind of miracle that I didn't jerk my rifle with just a little flinch and blow the fevered brains right out of Alverez's head.

But I didn't. Yet as it turned out, it would have required some other kind of miracle to send a signal through the squinting eyes and frenzied brains behind the perimeter wire to their itchy trigger fingers and tell them to stop firing and trying to annihilate what must have obviously appeared before them, in stark silhouette, with helmets and flak jackets, firing *away* from the perimeter, into the area of the unintentional ambush, as friendlies and fellow Marines. But they didn't. They didn't stop firing. And I can't explain how it was that we hadn't already been hit. And I am not really sure whether it was the reckless closeness of the rounds I was hurling past his head, the proximity of the last M79, or if he had just finally run out of juice. But something switched the lever in his head back to sane and Alverez stopped firing, crouched down, spun around and scrambled back to my location. We crouched down, reloaded and continued firing.

It was this maneuver that seemed to have sprung up out of thin air. A sort of leap frog. And we worked our way back to Johnson who had not stopped firing the whole time except to reload. Moving one at a time until once again we were all three together and we were alive and not one of us had been hit.

Somehow this thought must have occurred to me but I really don't remember it. Because things just seemed to turn black about that time. The one thing I do remember and what sticks out so bright in my mind is *the ring of fire*. Yeah, it sounds like a Johnny Cash song. But this is exactly what happened.

We made a dash for the perimeter. Well not really a dash but more like a slosh because it is hard to run in rice paddies. The mud at the bottom would suck off your boots if they weren't tied on good. There must have been a lull in the firing from the perimeter and we must have figured that they had finally recognized us. What with the lit up spectacle we had provided for them only moments before. But we figured wrong.

And I remember that when we were crossing the first rice paddy, just before the dike that separated it from the paddy closest to the wire, my helmet went flying off. Maybe it was from the jarring motion of what felt to me like running in quicksand or maybe from a bullet. Incredibly I actually stopped, turned back, recovered the helmet from its shallow watery grave and put it back on. But it wouldn't remain there long. Because as I quickly turned and continued charging toward the dike with enough momentum to get my right foot and leg up onto it in order to propel myself over and into the next rice paddy, my helmet flew off again.

This time I didn't go back for it. In fact, I never went back for it. It could still be lying there below the surface imbedded in the mud and the muck to this very day for all that I know. Because what happened when I reached the dike and flung my right foot up and out of the sucking grip of the paddy to the higher and drier surface and as my forward motion and my center of gravity and my right leg all worked in consortium to lift me up on top, my helmet popped off again and I was looking directly into the line of fire of an M60 machine gun coming from less than one hundred meters away, perhaps fifty and the gunner had his sights trained directly onto me and although I don't know if anyone would believe this it is exactly what happened.

I could see the bullets and I could feel them rushing by. Some of them less than inches and they were like a circle of little red lines of light coming towards me. A ring of fire. And I was in the middle of it. What I did without stopping, without thinking, except for a momentary flash of utter resignation and the basic survival instinct to save my sorry ass, was I dove head first through the center of the burning ring of fire and I went down like a stone into and under the surface of the shallow depths of the rice paddy on the other side of the dike. With my rifle jammed muzzle end first into the muck below I grabbed and clutched with both hands the roots and stocks of the underwater rice plants and I didn't care how little air I had in my burning lungs and pounding brain. I wasn't going back up there. I clung to the bottom closer than a bug to the surface of a windshield on a speeding automobile. I would, of course, eventually but not until the idiot behind the M60's trigger finger got tired or somebody yanked him off of it.

All the while this was happening, I had no idea what was happening with Johnson and Alverez. By the time that I could hear that the firing above had finally died down and I raised my head partially above the surface of the water with a gasp like the first breath of birth, I could see Johnson and Alverez nearing the gate of the perimeter wire, which really wasn't a gate per se, but a spot where the wire could be temporarily separated and there was someone there doing just that and they were no longer shooting at us.

When we got inside the wire we were by this time, as you might imagine, completely crazed. Without so much as a *howdy do* to the 13th Marines who had let us in, we were already, the three of us, tripping and scrambling with a marked determination towards the compound of the 26th Marines where all of the firepower had been coming from. We were tripping and scrambling because of the clumsiness of the added weight of a number of our own 13th Marines who were clinging to various appendages of our enraged and inconsolable Marine Corps bodies.

I am not exactly sure of what it was we were hell-bent set on doing. But it was something in the general area of rape, plunder and pillage. If you substituted *rape* with *murder* and then something happened that just sucked the wind right out of our sails and cut us off at the knees. I don't know how many times they said it before the words which I am sure were spoken, yelled and screamed in very plain English finally penetrated our maniacal revenge obsessed skulls. But there it was: "They didn't pass the word to the second watch that an LP was out there! They didn't know."

And with that and this is just like it was out of a movie, a couple of older sergeants gently as possible sat us down on the sandbag wall of a bunker and stuck cigarettes into our mouths and lit them as our hands and fingers were still incapable of such a subtle activity. And they cooed and calmed us and stroked us back into the world of the almost sane and then someone came running down and told us that the CO wanted us to report to him ASAP and so we did. But on the way I stopped at the armor's shack who was, of course, like everybody else very much awake and I asked him if he would clean my M16 because the barrel was packed with mud from my little swan dive into the rice paddy and this is what he said: "Just shoot the fucker up into the air about ten rounds. That'll clear it out." So that's exactly what I did. And I imagine everybody in the compound raised off the deck an inch or two but I didn't care. I thought it was funny how even though it was always said that a grain of sand could blow the barrel of an M16 if you didn't get it out of there, this unorthodox method of clearing it didn't hurt it at all. Of course, I cleaned it up good as soon as I got the chance.

Anyway, so the three of us go up to see the CO and he tells me to report. So I give him the rundown on what had happened and how it went and all of that and then something really strange happened. In fact, it is one of the strangest events that I have ever been a witness to. I am still not really sure of how it could have happened. First, when I was finished with the report, the CO said this: "Alright Corporal Thompson." (*even though I was still a Lance Corporal*) "Good job men. I want you to take a fifteen minute breather and then I'm sending you back out there."

I'm not kidding. That is what he said. But that isn't the weird part. The strange thing was that although it was still dark, I looked over and I could see on the faces of Alverez and Johnson the same *oh shit, you've got to be kidding me* look that I could feel on my own face and what distinctly appeared to be and what I knew to be, the *F-Position* forming on their mouths. You know, the Bucky Beaver look.

But you couldn't say those things to a Lieutenant Colonel. Especially your own Commanding Officer. Even though it had to be totally clear that the three of us going back out there alone after what had just happened would be crazy. Suicidal. But you also couldn't refuse an order from the CO. And he seemed to be excited by the fact that we had made contact with the enemy. Even though that wasn't really our mission. Or was it? Anyway, he seemed to want some more of it. But then of course, he wouldn't be going out there with us. And I slapped my left hand over Alvarez's mouth.

And that's when it happened.

Right out of the black. The **Old Man** stepped forward. He must have been a good two feet shorter than the CO who I remember wore size 13 and 1/2 boots that had to be special ordered. And the **Old Man** looked like a rock. Square jawed. With a wizened look that absolutely exuded everything hallowed, sacred, sad and glorious about the indescribable soul and history of the Corps. And the effect was immediate. He was a Sergeant Major. Not just *a* Sergeant Major, but, as I would later find out, *the* Sergeant Major. *The Senior Sergeant Major of the entire United States Marine Corps.* And I figured he had at least a thousand years in the Corps and had been in every battle since the Revolution. But at the time, I had absolutely no idea he was there in our camp, where he came from, who he was, or where he went after that brief encounter at the top of our hill in the dark heat of another mainly forgotten and anonymous night under the black and starless skies of Vietnam.

But I did know that the Sergeant Majors held the highest enlisted rank in the Green Machine and were the harbingers of the true spirit and traditions of the undying Corps and were revered if not feared by Senators, Congressmen and Generals alike. And that nobody messed with them. And if you saw one on a parade deck he would practically need a wheelbarrow to carry all of the ribbons and medals and that they were all actually earned. And at the very moment the CO, who I am sure had some very good reasons for doing so, ended with the words: "...and then I'm sending you back out there", the *Old Man*, who must have been standing behind the CO and had listened to the brief exchange between myself and the Lieutenant Colonel, seemed to simply materialize before us. Right out of space and time. And without any hesitation he turned, planted his feet firmly against the ground and faced the CO. (I swear you couldn't have knocked the Old Man over with a bulldozer). And this is what he said:

"Sir, with all due respect, you aren't sending *my men* back out there again tonight."

There was no response. You could have heard a pin pulled a mile away. And then he dismissed us. And we tip-toed backwards as soundlessly as we could and faded into the dark and safe obscurity of our hunkered down brothers on the perimeter. And we left them standing there on that night on that hill and around us all was still and all was quiet. And I never heard another word spoken about it. Almost as if it never happened. But it did.

The next morning a guy who worked in the dark and secretive communications bunker with the eerie glowing green computer screens came out of his dank lair blinking and scratching, lit a smoke and casually told me that they had picked up seventeen moving figures on their radar screen during the time of our LP. All of them close together at our location. They had watched it all unfold like a silent video game. Up until that moment, I didn't even know that we had radar.

The old need to know thing.

THE LETTER

I remember I was sitting on the rough wooden steps of the S1 Admin hooch in my fading green camouflage rain washed utilities. The zipper on my pants was already beginning to rust. On one side of me the terrain went down gradually to the perimeter, the abandoned rice paddies, the bush and dry ground area, the ridge and then Da Lai Pass. On the other side was a large black smudge that used to be my hooch. My rifle and ammo were within arm's reach. I don't know who I got the clothes from but it was a real pleasure to be just sitting there in the sun doing absolutely nothing. It was about a week or so after the attack. I'm not really clear on that but I do remember there was a really sad atmosphere in the camp. It hadn't been long. You could easily see the tension in people and we were still on close to one hundred percent alert and would be for some time to come. Our mess hooch was practically gone and so were our cooks. We ate C Rats. Things had changed and it would be a couple of months before a sort of normalcy would return. But it would never be like it was before.

And then out of the corner of my eye I saw him coming. A guy I didn't know very well. Sandy had come by earlier, delivered the mail and had already gone back to An Hoa. I didn't get anything but I really didn't care. I didn't want anyone to know what had happened anyway. Especially my mother. My dad had died a couple of years before. But it was nice to see Sandy. I must have been called up for some kind of admin thing and I was done with it and just sort of doing the *shit bird* thing. Which meant I was avoiding laying wire or filling sandbags, digging holes, or whatever. And that was just fine with me. Then I saw him out of the corner of my eye.

He was walking and holding a letter way up close to his face. Like he was near-sighted or something. And like all at once he does this

138

incredible thing. He looks at the letter, looks up and then he looks at the letter again. I figured he must have done that about a million times already as he walked up the trail and approached the spot that I was sitting at on the steps. All of a sudden, right in front of me, he just drops the letter like it was some kind of poison or something. His hands go up to his head and he just starts to scream.

It's like nothing I've ever heard before. And it practically scared the shit right out of me. I'm not kidding. Then without hesitation, he throws himself headlong into the brand-new roll of barbed concertina wire we had just laid along the front of the hooch whose steps I was sitting on. And he is thrashing and flailing himself in the razor sharp wire and all the while making the most god-awful sound imaginable. Cutting himself up like crazy. Like that was just exactly what he wanted to do. Of course, I am already on my feet and on the way down and I holler over to two other guys who are nearby. It takes all three of us to wrest him from the barbed quagmire he was enmeshed in and he never cooperated a bit.

After they dragged him away and I later heard that he was sent to a psychiatric hospital in Bethesda, Maryland, or something like that, I reached down and picked up the letter and I held it up close to my face. It was a very short letter. In fact, it was only one sentence long. And not a very long sentence at that. And this is what it said:

"Your baby is dead and I'm leaving you."

MAMASON

It was just another **MEDCAP** mission to a village whose name I can't recall. There were only six of us Marines and we were spread out so far around the perimeter of the ville that I remember we couldn't even see each other and I was just standing there in the open and I knew now that I was utterly vulnerable, exposed and that anything could happen from anywhere and at anytime.

It was like the feeling I got a couple of days before when I was on a patrol back at the camp out by the ridge and I was walking through some bush that was black and withered and the only way that I can describe it is that it was slimy, like a million snails had oozed across every leaf of every bush and turned them black and shriveled in their wake and the slime was getting all over me. Especially the exposed skin on my arms which always seemed to have a lot of long thin cuts on them. Like paper cuts. They were caused by the bush. I had a particular problem with the jungle rot, which just seemed to take to me like I was a particular prime piece of Scotch Irish Scandahoovian Minnesota White Meat. That simply cried out to the fungicidal life of Southeast Asia and said:

"Eat me!"

And so I could feel the sting of the slime as I gingerly walked through the bush. I remember thinking: "This must be Agent Orange" and that is when I noticed it. And I froze. Less than one inch from the left side of the toe of my right boot was the head of a small plunger that looked like a nail. What I knew immediately to be the detonator of a mine. A landmine. And before my heart began to beat again I looked back at my other foot and within about a half inch from the heel of that boot was another one. And I stayed froze. Every bone, tendon, muscle and cell had come   to   a   complete   stop.

Even my lungs. And I don't really know how I did it. That is come to a complete stop. Because of my forward motion. But I did. And I didn't move. Not for awhile anyway. And it proved to me the theory of suspended animation. But most importantly, how utterly vulnerable I was. And how Agent Orange had saved my legs and probably my life. I never would have seen the plungers if the leaves had not been shriveled up. So I marked the spot with a flare parachute and left it for EOD* guys to deal with. A job I didn't envy.

But what really got to me was how easy it was to lose a limb. And I had seen it. It's worse looking at than even death. You just can't imagine it unless you see it. I'm not going to try to describe it. I mean what for? You can't imagine it.

Well anyway, this is where my head was at when we were guarding the doctor in the village that particular day. I couldn't see the Marine to the left or to the right of me and I was pretty much just looking all over the place at the same

*(EOD - Explosives Ordinance Disposal.)

time until the mamason came out of nowhere out in front of me. She was coming my way like she was going to invite me in for a cup of tea or something. Except for the look on her face. Which just kind of hit me right in the gut as soon as I saw it. The mamason looked crazed. I mean really crazed. Demented. Like she had just escaped from an insane asylum. And she seemed to be in a hurry. In a hurry to come to me. And my rifle and my trigger finger were way ahead of me. They were pointing right at her head. While I was still looking at her face.

You couldn't help it.

Right away she looked older than she probably was. She had a sort of crazy grin-like expression that looked like a grin one second and a grimace the next. Or somehow both even at the same time. She was rapping away to beat the band, but of course I couldn't understand any of it. Then I saw her hands. They were fumbling around at her clothing up by her chest and she had a baggy loose fitting garment on, wrapped together like a robe, with a cord at the waist and she was kind of chunky. My eyes were going from her face to her hands, to her face and to her hands and she was

144

still squawking away in an excited and high pitched way. Coming right at me.

Her hands finally found the fold that she had been fumbling for and I am screaming over and over whatever it was that I thought would mean "stop", or "go away" in Vietnamese. I might as well have been talking Martian or saying: "C'mon mamason, c'mon and just kill the hell out of me." Because the mamason wasn't about to stop. She was coming right at me and she wasn't going to stop for nothing. Not unless I pulled the trigger.

And it seemed when I was looking into her face that I was looking at the face of the war. From an old mother's point of view. What had happened to her family? What happened in the village at night? After the doctor, the interpreter and the Marines went away? But I swear she didn't look right and she was going to pull something she had strapped to her chest, or pull something out like a satchel charge with a *No Second* delay on it and then parts were going to start flying. Some of them mine.

But I didn't do the right thing. The smart thing. The thing that every voice in my frightened screaming brain kept telling me to do. And at last no more than three feet before me she came to a halt. And with a wide and opened jaw her maniacal grin fully exposing her heavily red stained teeth and with trembling jerks of her pudgy wrinkled fingers, succeeded in unfolding the soiled clump of old rag she had extracted clumsily from the fold in her shirt. And she held it out in front of her. Right up to my face. Like an offering.

It was beetle nut. Just an old rag full of beetle nut. The mild narcotic nut that a lot of the older mamasons seemed to like to chew. It was a natural sedative and came in red or black and after they chewed it that is what color their teeth and mouths became. It was quite a sight. And that is what was looking up at me and I swear my finger must have gone into spasms for the rest of the day because it was like a million pound weight was pressing on that finger to pull the trigger on my M16 and blow that crazy mamason to hell. But it is the singularly most important thing I *didn't* do while I was in Vietnam.

MAMASON

I have always known and it seemed so close to have gone either way and everyone would have said that I "didn't have a choice".

But I would have opened up the rag afterwards. I would have seen what was inside it. And I would have seen that face and that crazy old mamason coming at me and I would have killed her over and over and over and over again and again in my mind for the rest of my life. And nobody would have known nothing about it.

But me.

THE YEAR OF THE RAT

Villages-hamlets-homes we visited

The author at a Pagoda

Lina

149

THE YEAR OF THE RAT

LINA

Pronounced: Leena

L ina was beautiful. Not just physically beautiful. She was that for sure. Slender, agile, light on her feet, she walked with grace. Sure footed. Almost cat like. She had delicate features, long black raven hair and bright alert eyes. And she was intelligent. Very smart, yet quick to smile or laugh when the mood was light. But at other times, quiet times, if you looked closely enough, you could see something else lingering there in the ebony sheen of her dark Asian eyes. Something far away...in the past or in the future. Or a mixture of both.

This was her Country, her Land, her People and her Life. We were passing through. Still, something about Lina made you want to reach out to her. To touch her. Hold her. Take her into your arms. To feel what's inside of her. But it wasn't like that. You didn't do it. Everybody liked Lina. Respected her. And everybody was on his best behavior around her. When Lina was around. And nobody had to tell you that. Tell you to knock it off. She didn't command respect – she earned it. Naturally. Even when she wasn't around, I don't remember anybody ever saying anything tasteless or vulgar about her. Not even jokingly. Never. And we were young. Hot blooded horny Marines. Are there any other kind?

Nobody put the moves on Lina. You may have wanted to. But more so, you wanted to be just sitting with her someplace clean and safe. Someplace quiet except for normal sounds. Normal smells. The breeze softly brushing her midnight hair. Moonlight flickering in her inquisitive eyes. Sharing a bottle of French wine and talking about Love and the meaning of Life. Or holding her hand while strolling barefoot on a sun baked beach. The azure waves dropping rhythmically on the soft yellow sand. Lina inspired good thoughts. Healthy thoughts. And she spoke French and English fluently. And of course, her own native Vietnamese and all of its various dialects. She was very bright, very professional and she was the Vietnamese Interpreter for the First Battalion, Thirteenth Marines.

Lina would accompany us on medcaps. She would interpret between the villagers and the American doctor while he attended to their various ailments. She was right there for the little kid with the tapeworm helping out with the extraction. She was a marvel but when we were on these missions she was all business. It was a delight to observe her at work. But most of the time as security we Marines were thinly dispersed around the village, spread out and consequently, much of what Lina did was shrouded in mystery. We didn't even know where she had come from when she showed up at our camp, who her family was or anything about her past. A black veil of anonymity drawn for her own security.

She wore tropical camouflage utilities like the rest of us and a bush hat creased at the sides and turned up in front showing her face. A little bit jaunty but befitting her confident forward looking personality. That is the only way I ever saw Lina dressed. Never in civilian clothes. But she looked sharp. She obviously had a better class of tailor and a much much more industrious launderer. A mystery wrapped in Indochina wrapped in Marine Corps tropical cammies.

We were thundering along on a red dirt road heading back to camp in the back open air bed of a truck. The driver, Lina and the doctor ensconced comfortably up front in the cab. We were coming back from another medcap at another ville, Lina and the doc probably ruminating on the particulars and peculiar rarities of the medical caseload administered to in the steamy open air day clinic in the village center. These were small poor rural villages of mostly individual thatched huts and family dwellings spread out amidst the native flora interconnected by an informal network of walking paths. It was just one such village which we had just left not too many minutes or miles before and I and five of my buddies were bouncing along in the back of the truck enjoying the breeze, a smoke and some fresh air.

Suddenly, the truck came to an abrupt stop. At the time, there had been no other traffic on the road. I don't recall seeing or passing any other vehicles on the road going out to the ville or returning. Not a one. Not up until that point. When the driver unexpectedly hit the break jolting us out of our private thoughts, our eyes and weapons hurriedly probing the now more intensified environment around us.

What the hell? You don't want to do that. Stop dead in the damn road. But the reason became quickly apparent. We weren't the only exposed target idling stupidly under the heavy heat of the mocking sun. Directly ahead, about seventy five yards, looking over the cab of the truck I saw what the driver saw. Why he had come to a sudden stop. A lone jeep motionless in the middle of a lonely road in the middle of nowhere. Facing the same direction as ourselves. Inside the jeep only one occupant, sitting in the driver's seat, back facing our direction. Seemingly oblivious to our presence. To being observed. And apparently oblivious to the enormous and obvious lethal risk and jeopardy he had placed himself in parked and isolated on this lonely stretch of road surrounded by a hostile and heartless predatory countryside.

Or was he already dead? Worse for him would have been that he was surrounded and captured alive. Beaten and trussed up with his wrists bound behind and roped tightly to a neck cinch, gagged and hurriedly jabbed and prodded into the unforgiving bush. A fate perhaps pitilessly prolonged or in any case mercilessly rendered with sheer unrelenting brutality. Swallowed up and absorbed into the bowels of a history that would in time be inclined to look the other way.

Captured enlisted men were not the political prizes that their skyward brethren the pilots were. Nor were they the intelligence bonanza that the airborne backseaters and electronics communication experts were. And although the aforementioned were treated horrendously and that for those that would eventually return their very survival was a testament to their unimaginable courage and undefeatable will to endure the unendurable, the captured enlisted men were simply expendable and were for the most part treated as such. After having rendered up to their captors their proverbial *pound of flesh*.

However, this was not the fate of our erstwhile loitering jeep pilot. Oh no. For although he appeared motionless from our relatively distant point of view, our seemingly incapacitated jeep jockey was not entirely devoid of activity. Although the activity, however subtle from such a distance, appeared to be centered and orientated somewhere and somehow in the general vicinity of his waist. Obscured from our line of sight but inferred by the undulating motions and rhythmic ministrations of the mobilized mamason crouched and bent forward lurching through the open front door of the jeep. Her head centered over the driver's lap. Bobbing...

Damn!

Lina. All that I could think about was Lina. Sitting there in the front seat of the truck. Wedged between the doc and the driver. Speechless. Unable to move. Staring. What was she thinking? Feeling? Embarrassment? Anger? Shame? Embarrassment as the only female in a truck full of Marines exposed to such a humiliating spectacle. Angry at the brazen and cavalier attitude of the clueless shitbird Marine. Ashamed and humiliated by the plight of her people and especially her gender exemplified in the degrading behavior of the genuflected mamason in the middle of the dirt road. In broad daylight. It was more than a matter of face.

Lina was a proud young woman. Justifiably proud. And although I wasn't with her inside the cab of the truck at the moment, I somehow felt I was there with her inside of her head. Inside her heart. And right now, that was not a comfortable place to be. Something had to happen.

Surprisingly, all is still and all is quiet in the back of the truck. No snickers, no guffaws or lewd commentary. Nobody was amused. A sense of shared sobriety permeated the electrified atmosphere. A sort of kindling ripe for the inclusion of a random spark to burst it into an unassailable and unaccountable violence. All of it directed at the now drunkenly gesticulating head of the slack jawed jeep jockey.

That is when it happened. Somehow without actually opening the door the good doctor, not a small man by any measure, had managed to extract the greater bulk of his being through the right passenger side window of the truck. Suddenly and somehow, with a firm grip on some part of the endoskeleton of the truck with his left hand, he extended his upper body and torso fully through and outside of the window in one deft movement into the open air somewhat like the explosive action of a slightly off kilter Jack In The Box and with his right hand, just as deftly, in one fluid motion drew with the rapidity of Zorro's glistening sword a hitherto unseen battery powered portable Megaphone to his pursed lips as if to kiss the saber's hand guard and with the amplification device activated, cut through the heavy anticipatory silence of the pregnant air with a startlingly hair raising electro static jolt, crackle, squelch and the following flame throated command:

"Get your sorry ass out of that jeep Marine! This is Captain Jack Bloodswell. STAND AT ATTENTION! NOW!!!"

Whoa...! Suddenly, the spring of mounting tension which had been wound to such an ominous constriction was sprung. And as the malingering Marine driver stumbled from the jeep over the shadow of the now halfway-to-Hanoi mamason (God knows, she could have been working for them) and as he hastily scrambled to cinch up his sagging utility pants, which kept dropping as he frantically attempted to come to some semblance of standing at a proper attention, the whole truck broke out into unrestrained rancorous belly bursting laughter. Yes, even the truck itself! And the laughter didn't stop when the God Almighty voice of the super charged doctor once again sliced the air. This time amidst the boisterous cacophony of hoots and hollers and in no uncertain terms commanded the panic stricken pecker pirate back to base and without haste.

As the thick cloud of road dust billowed up in pale red plumes behind the urgently departed galloping jeep and amidst the now waning revelry, coughs and comical commentary, I could hear clearly the colorful knee slapping laughter of Lina's lovely melodious almost sing song voice. Its magical modulations filling the cab as we began to roll emanating outward above the groan of the gears and tired grumble of the aging engine, unhappy to have been awakened from its unanticipated rest, into the farms, hamlets and small villages off the road.

LINA

The desultory wizened eye of an old water buffalo casting a furtive glance as we rumbled by. Lina still laughing. Just another day in the countryside.

And she was laughing in Vietnamese.

THE YEAR OF THE RAT

Aerial shots from helicopters

155mm tank firing from An Hoa Combat Base

(Alpha Battery 1/13)

THE YEAR OF THE RAT

ELEPHANT VALLEY

I don't know much about it. But I've always really liked the name. Elephant Valley. Right away you just know that there had to be elephants in it. At least once upon a time. But I don't remember anyone ever talking about that. Which seems really odd when you think about it. Because of the name. But that's just the way things were. You were never really told much about what was happening. Especially if you were a clerk corporal going along as a *warm body* and a worker bee on a mission to put a 105mm howitzer firebase on the tip of a mountain which looked over a river valley to the west and onto other mountains, in a range of mountains, which I was told when we got there were located in a place and a country called Laos. But to tell you the truth, I don't really know where I was. It was called: "Operation Campbell Streamer" and it was out in grunt country to the north and then further north and west of Danang and it took quite a while to get there by helicopter. I was in the last of six choppers whirling their way at a high rate of speed high above the dark and mysterious serpentine valley below. Like an aerial convoy of Trojan elephants following trunk-to-tail, one after another, over the early morning mist rising off the floor of the ancient elephant trail.

To me it was unbelievable. And at the same time like nothing. Utter resignation. It was happening and I couldn't stop it. You were just there. And I mean how could I refuse Captain Smiley's offer? "Hey, Tommy. You've got three weeks left in Country. You go on this operation and you'll be gone no more than one week, I'll cut your orders the day you *git* back."

Whoa! I mean it wasn't hard to do the math. No matter how you cut it, I would be getting on the *Big Bird* at a minimum two weeks early. And my *short time calendar* was already closing in on the Big Three. If I went, when I got back, I could fill out fourteen segments of the tattered but luscious goddess that someone somewhere had crudely yet lovingly sketched out.

A naked goddess sketched out in a bold, complementary, single line fashion, accentuating particularly voluptuous anatomical parts. With limited detail. Save for a warm and inviting expression on her come-hither face. Then by line had broken up the composite form into one hundred small segments that numbered down to one. I will leave it to your analytical powers of perception to deduce the location and destination of the last three precious and intensely longed for final numbers. We took particular pleasure in carefully shading in the individual segments. Starting on the periphery of the elusive dream girl. One hundred days before going *back to the World*. You were lucky if your mimeographed shortime dreamgirl calendar even survived. Just from the elements and the repetitive folding and unfolding. And the rains. You just can't imagine the rain. You always kept your calendar with you like it was a sacred object. Usually in the upper chest pocket over the heart. And filling it out was something that you usually wanted to do alone if you could manage it. Almost like a sexual thing. And that is probably about where my mind was at when Captain Smiley sprung open the screen door of the S1 Admin hooch. Stepped out onto the front step and made the proposal.

To go or not to go?

I was lucky. Most guys wouldn't have had a choice. But I couldn't blame Captain Smiley. I had three weeks left and I had already become a *shit bird*. I think for my position it was at least one week too early. I could have maybe stretched it out for a couple of weeks but as it was, I had already become sort of useless and in the middle of the day I was just lying there in my tiger shorts sunbathing on the top of a sandbag bunker. Listening to rock and roll and Hanoi Hanna from a transistor radio. In retrospect you could say I was just inviting unwanted attention. But like I say, I had been lucky and I was sort of pissed because for the last couple of nights while on perimeter watch, I had spotted movement up on the side of the ridge. I had verified it even in darkness through the *Starlight Scope* which allowed you to sort of see at night. Human figures moving in an artificial pale green light.

Like ghosts slithering through a liquid phosphorescent environment. With wispy shadowy tongues of black flame tracing off behind them. And I looked. I blinked. Rubbed my eye and I looked again. They were still there and I called it in.

The next night I saw them again and I called it in again. Nothing happened. In the morning I did a crazy thing. After my watch I went up to the Command Post and told them what I had seen for the second night in a row. How both times I had called it in to the Corporal of the Guard and how nothing was being done about it. And how I figured that they were moving a cache of mortars or something in and I actually said: "Let me take a couple of guys up there and see what's going on." They said: "No." It seemed strange. Why not? If I was stupid enough to want to go up that ravine four or five hundred meters, on a very steep incline, against what I expected to be a buried cache of weapons or a dug-in NVA mortar crew, with an obvious high ground terrain advantage, why should they stop me? But they did. Like I say, I was lucky. It was like somebody was looking out for me. In spite of myself.

Like the time not too long before when I was sitting alone in the middle of the day on a sandbag bunker on the perimeter. It was a dry bright sunny day and I was just sitting there with my helmet off soaking it up looking out towards *The Pass*. But my thoughts were like a million miles away and then *zip*. Just like that. My daydream was blown away. Faster than *a frog fart in a hurricane*.

The sniper's bullet passed no further than half an inch from my left temple. Right above my ear. I felt it as much as heard it. If I had even the average amount of hair that my peer group was sporting back in the World, the bullet would have burned a tunnel right through it. And if there had been or there had not been just the slightest breeze blowing in the right direction between where I was sitting and where the sniper had launched the shot, the bullet instead of passing harmlessly past my left temple and over the tip of my left ear, would have instead driven a tunnel directly through my forehead. Through my brain.

And out the back of my skull. I was off the top of the bunker and hugging the inside of the hole before the sound of the shot had even reached me. Well let's just say I didn't hang around up there waiting for it. So anyway, I said *Yes* to the operation. And I told myself it was to get out two weeks early but I think there was more to it than that.

"Phu phu phu phu phu phu...." The sound of a chopper does something to your brain. I don't know what it is but whatever it is, it sticks with you. Like an odor. When you hear it, it brings things back. Like the sudden waft of a fragrance recalls not just the memories of your childhood, but the actual atmosphere that you experienced them in. And can even reach into and through the dark void and empty blackboard of amnesia. Like a bookmark. It takes you right back to where you left off. And after we lifted off, the vibratory effect of the twirling rotors chopping away at the heavy air syncopated with our tumbling thoughts and we were off. *The Magical Mystery Tour.* Don't get me wrong - we were scared shitless. What the hell was I doing? I had volunteered. What had happened to my *True North*?

171

There was just something about that Captain Smiley. How could I refuse him? He had been good to me. He got my promotion and put me in for the medal that I didn't think I deserved. Yeah, I had worked long hours and did all the real stuff that was asked of me, but I didn't *volunteer* for any more LP's like Johnson and Alverez did. They were good guys and you could count on them. I learned that the hard way. But we never talked about it.

And Captain Smiley had been bitten by the Rat. Oh, you didn't want that. I can't say that enough. I remember when I first got down in Country. Some guys telling me about a patrol that went out in the area shortly before I arrived and one guy had stopped to relieve himself in the bush. And how when he was taking a leak, a six or seven inch centipede jumped or was shaken out of the bush and on the way down the giant bug had clung to and had bitten him on his most forward projecting member. It bit him on his point man!

Down he went. Writhing and screaming in agony. They said that his penis swelled from the effects brought on by the poisonous centipede's

172

venom to the point where the skin actually split apart. And you can only imagine as I did, what that experience must have been like for that unhappy Marine on a routine patrol and what it must have been like when he was medivaced, treated by and passed through the able hands of a long unbroken chain of U.S. Naval medical personnel? From the corpsman in the field and on the medivac chopper, to the specialists on the hospital ship or the emergency surgical field hospital by the airfield on the outskirts of Danang.

And all of the doctors, interns, nurses, orderlies and administrative types that would have been helplessly drawn, whether by professional interest, duty, or concern, or by a simple and overpowering voyeuristic curiosity, to the unusual case and particular plight of the young wounded warrior. Who, while exercising his assigned duties to his unit, Corps and Country was suddenly, unexpectedly and cruelly felled by a vicious and toxic attack. Executed through the deployment of the stealthful arts of subterfuge, camouflage, concealment, ambush and ultimately the secretious chemical warfare of an enormous and wily Southeast Asian Bug. Only to face the

173

dreaded and ineluctable question awaiting his return back home. From family, friends, acquaintances and perhaps even his hometown newspaper:

"Where did you get hit?"

Oh, and I suppose there would have to be the inevitable snickering follow-up questions: "Did you get a Purple heart?" "Can I see your scars?" "Did the Viet Bug get away?" "Were you shooting at him when he attacked you or did you run out of ammo?" Well you can just imagine. He never did return and I never did hear the story being passed on to any other new guys. So it didn't appear to be just another jungle myth. Maybe the Stars and Stripes sent a reporter and a photographer out to interview him before he left Country, but I doubt it. Anyway he should have become a legend and maybe he did. I sure hope things came out all right for him in the end.

So there I was. Sitting in the last of the six choppers heading west by northwest with about a dozen other pensive Marines with our weapons and our eighty pound packs, including twenty pounds of C4 plastic explosives each. And nobody was saying a word. Except for the silent words and images that were pulsating through our brains and, of course, everybody is thinking about different things. And it's hard to be actually thinking about nothing. I don't know what the others were thinking about but I was thinking about the Rat. The Rat that had bitten Captain Smiley. The important thing was not to be thinking too much about where you were going. That much seemed pretty clear. But I wasn't exactly clear about how Captain Smiley got bit.

What I remember, and what sticks out so vividly, is watching him every morning for fourteen days take out this orange juice size glass. And I don't know where he got it because we drank out of our steel canteen cups, but anyway, he would take out this bottle of bourbon and fill the glass. I figured it was about six or eight ounces of good Kentucky Bourbon and that he had most likely purchased it in Danang or at the 1st Marine Division PX. That is if they even sold liquor. But I didn't envy him or ever once even contemplate raiding his stash. Not for even one swig. Even though the one and only bottle of hooch that I was able to acquire as an enlisted man, a quart bottle of Seagram's VO for which I splurged and paid two U.S. dollars for instead of the dollar eighty for the lesser grade Seagram's 7, was a casualty along with Chesty, the corpsman and everything else I owned in the world. And it wasn't even a third empty. The bottle that is.

So anyway, Captain Smiley would come out of his corner in the S1 Admin hooch which was the only area inside the hooch that had a partition and he would have the strangest look on his face and every morning for fourteen days first thing he would stop, stand there, finish pouring the bourbon into the glass and then for a moment he would stare. Right through the wood and screen outside wall of the hooch. Right through the hooch next to it. Right through the hill itself. And right through the war. And he would raise the glass up to his lips and drink the whole thing down clean. Then without a word being said, Captain Smiley would walk out through the back screen door of the hooch and take the long walk up the little hill to a little shed that was being used as a medical station and the corpsman would stick a long needle into his stomach or lower abdominal area one time each day, making what eventually became a perfectly shaped upright oval. Sort of like a big Easter egg consisting of from the most recent shot - *and they were deep shots* - a golf ball size lump leading the pack of the previous days lumps around his bellybutton like a slow meteorite circumnavigating Captain Smiley's navel. It was a hell of a thing to watch.

So I wasn't surprised when he asked me to go.

When we got to the valley that ran below the mountain that we were to scale the other five choppers had already dumped their loads into the tall elephant grass of the valley below. Like I say, I was in the last chopper. The other five had seemingly disembarked their passengers without incident and the lurching line of stooped over Marines was already approaching the base of the mountain. When we had initially arrived at the drop-off area the chopper pilots directed their improbable aircraft into an expansive circular pattern high above the wind tossed shimmering grassy valley and one by one descended into the emerald embrace of the vegetal world below, but they didn't actually touchdown. Instead they hovered four to six feet off the surface of the uncertain ground. The ten foot tall elephant grass waved about furiously and was eventually overcome by the downdraft of the rotors. Temporarily splayed out in a flattened disk like depression from the center as the heavily weighted occupants spilled out of the posterior ends of the buzzing mechanical flying insects. Spilled out like larval eggs into the soft fermented earth of the steamy valley floor.

But now it was our turn to evacuate the belly of the hovering beast and as I had been one of the first to board, I would be one of the last to disembark. In fact third from the last. And just when the fourth from the last, who was as I am sure you have deducted, immediately in front of me, outstretched his right leg and foot into the empty air outside the rear exit of the hovering helicopter to commence his short drop to the unmoving ground below, that is when it happened. And of course it just had to happen.

We started taking fire from the wood line on the opposite side of the narrow valley from where the already landed Marines from the other five choppers were located. And the door gunner of our own chopper, the one I was watching, was simply going bananas.

I had been watching him intensely and studying his amazing mannerisms as we swiftly descended into the womb of the valley below and I was utterly spellbound by what I saw. It was artistry. He was like one with his trade. With his weapon. One creature. Tethered to his swiveling M60 rapid fire machine gun by a harness. A two way radio communication cable ran from his helmet headset to the pilots and a continuous belt of M60 ammo fed into his rapacious weapon which darted back and forth back and forth like a nervous guard dog. As if it was almost alive.

And just exactly at the moment the *fourth to the last* extended his right foot off and out from the lip of the rear gate, the enemy opened up from the tree line on our chopper and the door gunner, who was already in a state of rabid frenzy, exploded. He just went berserk. But it was a controlled berserk. He was firing left to right left to right back and forth going up and down and up and down covering a large grid with hot lead hurled at high velocity. And as he was doing this and just when the *fourth from the last* was extending his leg for a four to six foot drop from the ass end of the chopper, the pilot jammed the controls into launch mode and we shot *straight up like a rocket.*

That is all of us except the *fourth from the last.* I watched him drop from at least thirty feet as we hurled into the heavens and he was just a speck when he hit the ground from my vantage point. I nearly tumbled after him from the force of the thrust and the vertigo caused by the sudden upward acceleration. After we had achieved a stable circling pattern high above the field of fire and the door gunner had returned to his normal state of frenzied calm, the copilot unplugged himself from his headset, stood up, walked directly back to where I was still standing in the rear of the chopper and yelled into my ear: "Shit, I'm sorry to say this, we'd take you right back to base but that guy over there has the radio and they need *it* on the ground."

Hmmmm......

I thought about what Captain Smiley had said. How as soon as I got back he would cut my orders. An evil thought immediately flooded my brain. I wanted to chuck that sucker, the radioman, right out of the back of the helicopter: "Why the hell wasn't he one of the first guys

out?" "Why was he in the end of the chopper?"
"Why the hell was he in *the last chopper*?"

It didn't make any sense. So after circling
around about a million miles up in the
stratosphere for I don't know how long, we went
back down. The door gunners were twitching
around all over the place. Like they had jumping
beans or hot coals in their pants and they set us
down alone. The three of us. *Alone.* In that
desolate valley. Before we had hardly hit the
ground the hitherto hovering chopper headed for
the heavens like a supersonic angel that had been
bit in the ass and was out of there like a backdoor
lover. I ain't never felt so alone in all my life as I
did that day. The hypnotic sound of the
homebound chopper faded away into oblivion and
left us there like naked schoolboys. Naked in
front of a jeering and giggling room full of high
school classmates.

But there we were. It was not a time for idle
contemplation. We picked ourselves up and we
soon caught up to the line heading up the
mountain. I remember as we trudged along that
there were large fortified caves and bunkers
owned by the NVA and as we passed between

them, Cobra gunships were sweeping down along the left and right of our line, firing rockets into the NVA emplacements. Swooping down like spitting snakes on either side of our meandering column at close quarters. Somehow it seemed like it was normal to be just walking along between the carnage, as the caves which were supported by large green logs were exploding and blowing to bits as the Cobras swooped and slithered close above our heads through the jungle canopy.

And then there was the mountain. I'm not going to tell you how hard it was to climb. God it was hot. And it was steep. And that radioman? He didn't make it. About halfway up with the worst part yet to go, he dropped like dead meat. We had to have him hoisted out on a rope, dangling from a medivac helicopter and he wasn't the only one. Then we got to carry the radio and his M16 the rest of the way up to the top, pulling ourselves along by grasping the roots and trunks of the brush and trees that clung precariously to the almost vertical embankment. I can't remember how many went down and were hoisted out, but most of the column made it to the top. It was exactly why I was glad that I wasn't a grunt.

I was never too fond of extreme physical pain. But nevertheless, I didn't wimp out and maybe I owed it to the training I had received back in the hills of Camp Pendleton California. When like all Marines I went through basic infantry training (ITR) except that I had along with the rest of my Company, the particular painful pleasure of falling into what we didn't know at the time was the infamous Oscar Company: "The Running O."

So named because absolutely every single place we ever went we ran. Before breakfast, breakfast, grenade range, three and a half miles each way with sixty pound packs and rifles. Down the desert hills of south California to, along and through the Pacific Ocean sands along the shoreline of the western sea. Where the Force Recon guys worked out. Sand is the worst thing to run in. You have to do it to know it. Anyway, we ran everywhere. All the time. You wouldn't believe it. The Corporal, the NCO that ran "O Company" was a track runner, a marathon man. And he wore jungle boots, tiger shorts, a green Marine short sleeve sweatshirt and he liked to run.

Like a deer. Of course he didn't care that we were weighed down like water buffaloes. Bloused utility trousers, leather boots, long sleeve shirts, rifles, packs, webbed utility belts with canteens. Whatever. All the equipment that we carried. And we carried it everywhere. And everywhere we went we ran. Even up "Suicide Ridge." A very steep swath of blood soaked dirt and rock worn lifeless by the constant scraping of knees and elbows and boots as we dragged our bodies, rifles, heavy machine-guns, mortar tubes, plates, ammo boxes, all of it to the top. Of course it was too steep to run but we were ordered to anyway.

The "Running O".

Oh it was splendid. The boxing matches and the cool California nights. When John O'Hanlan and I would sing <u>A Day in the Life,</u> by the Beatles, with an old acoustic guitar and a music book we somehow got a hold of. And I don't know what had ever happened to John O'Hanlan. He was a big tough handsome Irish guy from Seattle and he was my squad leader in boot camp. When he arrived at the Marine Corps Recruit Depot in San Diego he had long hair down to his ass and a beard and a mustache. The barbers who shaved our heads down to the skull had a little fun with him. They shaved off everything but his mustache. Leaving him looking a bit like Poncho Villa for the benefit of the DI's, who immediately took a special interest in him.

If there was one thing I learned in boot camp, it was that you did not want to stick out. But John O'Hanlan stuck out. And he suffered exponentially for it. But he consequently displayed great leadership potential and became a squad leader. Love was his undoing. It was the one thing you couldn't fault a Marine for. At least I didn't. He definitely wasn't a coward.

I once saw and mostly heard him do over eleven hundred squat thrusts. Right outside our boot camp Quonset Hut door. In the sandpit. It was punishment for some inconsequential, petty, fabricated or imagined crime, committed by the platoon as a whole. And the four squad leaders paid the price. Except listening to their tortured voices was unbearable torment to the rest of us. Sitting and *relaxing* inside our hut. Commanded to sit silently and polish our boots and brass buckles. I still do not like to think about it. After three or four hundred squat thrusts something happens to the human voice. And we always had to count them out. But this time we had to just sit and listen. And listen we did.

It always started with one hundred. And then when we got to the nineties you could always count on Gunnery Sergeant Marino, our senior drill instructor to say: "Stop, stop, stop. OK ladies, we don't like to count together. From the beginning, squat thrusts, two hundred of them, *readeeeeeey* - begin."

And this would go on and on and periodically the Gunny would step out of his Quonset Hut with his coffee and cigarette and then just about the time when we had almost reached the end he would come back out and then it would be three hundred and the whole thing would start all over again. But that would not be the end of it. Oh no. Somewhere on our way to three hundred, towards the end, out he would come again and with a stern look on his gopher like bulldog face, which never really changed much for the thirteen weeks our platoon was in boot camp, in his characteristically pinched nasal voice, he would say: "Stop, stop, stop ladies. Private Miller doesn't like to do squat thrusts with the rest of the platoon. Perhaps Private Miller has other things on his mind. So why don't we start again. From the beginning. Altogether... Ready? Squat thrusts to infinity! Begin!!!"

And then he would go back in and probably drink about a gallon of coffee. And as the sound of our voices and the cadence of our counting would trail off into and beyond the realms of insanity, eventually he would step back out of his hut and from a distance he would just stand there and gaze upon the miserable spectacle before him. One of his own making. His own creation. And if you looked hard enough through the torrent of sweat cascading down across and into your eyes, you could *almost* see through the shade cast by the visor of his Smoky The Bear DI hat a faint furtive hint of sad repose in the Gunny's steely eyes. Just before he would turn abruptly, without a word and reenter the comforts of his hallowed, corrugated sanctuary.

But things were not too comfortable in our hooch as we listened helplessly to the strangled voices emanating from the *sound holes* of John O'Hanlan and the other three delirious Squad Leaders in the sand pits outside our door. And the guilt was rising slowly like a dead rat up our sorry silent throats as the Squad Leaders choked out the endless count.

Something was going to happen if it didn't end soon. It was harder to listen to it than to do it yourself.

No, O'Hanlan wasn't a coward. But when he read that letter, the letter from his girlfriend and the ultimatum between sweet sweet love and the Corps and a ticket to Vietnam, it was just too much for the love struck Irishman. Off he went.

Right after ITR and I never saw him again. And I missed him. But I always figured they would catch him. They were very good at that and I saw AWOL* Marines dragged back in chains and leg irons when I was working nights for a couple of months in Staging Battalion. Right before I went through myself. It was not a pretty sight.

The AWOL's were not treated nicely to say the least and the very first place they would look for them was with their wives or girlfriends, right

*(AWOL - Absent Without Leave)

back in their hometowns. It was easy. And I always wondered what happened to that Westcoast Irishman. And every time I hear that song I think about him. I hope he fared well.

But the mountain wasn't easy. By the time we reached the top the eighty pound packs felt like we had found and carried the elusive Elephant Valley elephants on our backs from the steamy floor of the valley all the way up to the small tree covered mountain summit.

The surface at the top was relatively flat, but only big enough for a small landing zone and the three or four 105 millimeter howitzers that would provide the firepower for the aerial firebase we were sent out there to construct. The first order of business was to establish a tight perimeter and then immediately afterwards to begin blowing out all the trees and stumps. Until that was accomplished, a helicopter would not be able to land. And of course, once the trees were gone there would be no shade.

So we were essentially changing an environment that was hot as hell to one that was hotter than hell. Then there were the emplacements for the cannons to be dug and all the clearing and leveling that needed to be done after the trees and stumps were removed. That kind of work, along with the blistering heat, uses up a lot of water and the only water we had was what we had left in the canteens we carried with us during the ascent. We had already used up most of that. You either used it or you dropped. And *therein lies the rub.* We would not be getting any additional water for the next three or four days and nights. During which time you would see guys sucking on their bone dry canteens over and over again. Tapping, rubbing and otherwise cajoling their impotent plastic flasks for just one more precious drop of the life sustaining fluid. And it didn't matter that we had the LZ cleared and prepared before the end of the first day. They wouldn't bring us any water. They wouldn't come out there. And we began to wonder why.

You did a lot of wondering. And it kind of set you up for a lifetime of wondering. Oh I know. People always said: "It don't mean nothin." But when you think about it, really think about it, if it don't mean *nothing*, then it had to mean

190

something. The old double negative thing. Like Sandy for instance. I mean he meant something.

You see there was something else I carried up that mountain. Besides my pack, rifle, the whisked away radioman's rifle and on and off the radio. It was Sandy. And I might as well tell you that as heavy as that other stuff was, it was nothing compared to Sandy.

You see, not long before I volunteered to go on the operation, you know, to get the *early bird* back home, I got the news. But Sandy didn't bring it this time. Somebody else did. And I think that might have been the time I drank the rubbing alcohol. Now don't get me wrong. I would have rather drank real liquor instead but I couldn't find any. And I tried. I tried real hard. I even went to one of my black buddies. The one who had a piano key grin like the Cheshire Cat in Alice In Wonderland.

He had a real mouthful of teeth and they weren't very straight either. But he didn't have any booze and when he didn't have any there wasn't any to be had. And then I saw the plastic bottle of rubbing alcohol on the board shelf above someone else's cot in my hooch. You know for disinfecting bug bites or jungle rot or something. And so I drank it. I know it wasn't smart. I mean I'm not crazy. But I was that night. Remember I didn't even do a full thirteen month tour in Vietnam having spent some time first in Okinawa. But Sandy did. Right down to and including the very last day. He was on his way from An Hoa to the airport by Danang with a bunch of other guys in the back of a six-by truck. I rode in those trucks and the drivers always went fast. Not just because of snipers but because they thought that if they did hit a mine, that by going fast, most of the explosion from the mine would hit the rear of the truck instead of taking all of it straight up through the cab, where they were sitting. I don't know if it ever really paid off for any of them, but whether it did or not, that isn't what happened.

What happened is hard to believe. If someone told you, even if you had been to Vietnam, you might just get that blank staring look on your face and not know what to say. Like it sounds just a little bit too far fetched. Or maybe like impossible or a one-in-a-million kind of thing. And maybe that is just exactly what it was.

But it did happen. Just like this. The gooks took an undetonated 500 pound American bomb and tinkered around with it somehow or another and they placed it toward the back of a trench. A trench that they dug at an angle directed upwards and towards the road. By igniting an explosive charge behind the bomb they successfully hurled all 500 pounds of it up and out of the trench from a significant distance and it traveled in a perfect arc.

The distance from the trench to the road. Timed exactly. Not close as in horseshoes. But *exactly*. And it landed, struck and exploded directly onto, into and against the speeding six-by with the driver and the shotgun sitting next to him and the other fifteen Marines in the back who were looking towards Danang and the Big Bird and the World. Towards Home.

Until they heard the thrust charge explode and turned their heads to the left off the side of the dirt road, up ahead. They saw it coming. Up and out of the bush. Then level off and then descend in a perfect arc timed exactly. And it met the truck and the truck met the bomb at the exact point where they came together up ahead on the road

193

on the way to Danang. To the airport. The Freedom Bird. The pretty stewardesses. On their last day. On their way home. Dead. All of them. Sandy. Dead.

The *wave*...

The beautiful California sun flecked golden crested wave. Curled over and disappeared forever. Into the dark and unforgiving sea. Lost. Gone forever. Lost.

And you might think that I was too sensitive or something. And that I was affected more than other guys. But the next day after drinking the rubbing alcohol and the next night, I was back on the perimeter and sometime after the long hours of black nothingness a loud explosion went off close by over in the 26th Marine's Compound.

The first thought that raced through my brain was that there was no preceding shriek or whirling sound that a rocket or mortar makes as it is coming in. So I thought that it had to be sappers and an internal demolition just like before. And it turned out I was half right.

I don't know if I was told to or if I just took off on my own, but I left my position at the wire and I ran along the perimeter in the darkness, over to the 26th Marines where the explosion had occurred only moments before. There I saw him on the side of the hill. He was perfectly spread out like he had been made up of Tinker Toys that someone had pulled apart. His arms and legs close by but completely separated from his head and torso.

Somebody had a flashlight trained on the scene and I was told that the dismembered Marine spread out on the hill before me had been testing the punctured hole in a two pound coffee can full of C4 plastic explosive with a blasting cap and that it was his intention to use the homemade bomb to kill his First Sergeant. But the friction of the blasting cap rubbing against the crude perforation of the puncture in the steel coffee can resulted in enough of an electrical charge to ignite the two pounds of C4. And I always wondered what kind of stupid look he had on his face. When he was twiddling that cap into the can. And after I learned what had happened and more so why it had happened, it was just like looking at dead meat. I felt nothing.

The heat and the lack of water were taking their toll. By the second day on the mountain the corpsman was treating people for heat exhaustion. The trees were gone and we were working on blowing the stumps and removing the debris. The engineers that had trucked along with us, about seven or eight of them, were handling the demolitions. The rest of us were working with picks, axes, chainsaws and shovels. The Captain in charge of the job was showing no signs of slowing down.

There seemed to be a sense of urgency. The only problem was, whatever his reasons were and he wasn't sharing them with us, is that by the second and into the third day we were using our shovels to dig trenches about the length and width of a casket and the Corpsman was burying guys that were alive but who had gone from heat exhaustion into the much more serious and potentially fatal condition of heat stroke. He covered them with the loose soil right up so that only their faces were poking through. To cool them down. Because with heat stroke, you just burn up from the inside. Without water. The Corpsman was doing everything he could.

It wasn't enough that I had it on just about every other part of my body, but I ended up with a nice case of jungle rot on and around my lips because I had the bright idea, in spite of the good possibility of being shot, of scrambling down the side of the mountain a little ways and pulling up some fairly succulent looking plants. Breaking off the ends of their roots and sucking on them for the minute amount of moisture that they might contain. And after looking long enough at the huge, cool and very wet river flowing through the deep valley below the one side of the mountain, that is just exactly what I did. Remember I never said I was an Einstein.

Anyway, that's how things were going and they weren't getting any better. At night we were rolling grenades down the steep sides of our newly claimed encampment. I didn't know if what I heard creeping up from below were Rock Apes or NVA. I really didn't. But the grunts seemed to be pulling most of the grenades and I had to figure that they knew what the hell they were doing. Needless to say, we didn't sleep. Not at night.

And during the day one of the grunts did a really dumb thing. Just for a little excitement. Although it was not intentional. I remember when the squad of grunts first arrived. It was late on the first day and they came up from a different side of the mountain than we had. They looked pretty ragged to me. I imagined that they had been out there in the area for some time. You could tell right away they didn't look fresh, but then again, I am sure that we didn't either when we first hit the top.

What really stuck out to me, is how the whole squad was riding the hell out of this one guy. It was merciless. They were all over his ass. Taunting and chiding him as they humped their way over the ridge and into the clearing.

He was a tall lanky dufuss looking sort of a guy and I got the feeling that there had to be a guy like this in just about every squad everywhere in Vietnam. To fill the need for and become the outlet and the focus of the other members frustration and abuse. Especially during and after a very hard hump. And so of course this was the guy that did the really dumb thing.

You see we had a lot of C4 and to heat up our C-Rats we would roll up a little ball of the C4 and place it in a little hole in the ground and light it to cook up a can of whatever it was we were going to eat. You could do this and the C4 wouldn't explode. It would just burn harmlessly and you could throw it around and nothing would happen. But just the slightest static charge or electrical current would set it off and blow you to hell.

What the dufuss guy did was get a bit careless and started a grass fire and it just so happened that there was a claymore mine placed previously in the grassy area that was burning and a claymore when it explodes has the force and equivalent effect of about a thousand shotgun shells. So somebody yells: "Claymore!" and everybody dives for whatever cover was available. It put a hell of a dent in our dinner. It became apparent to me why the grunts were so irritated by this guy. The dufuss. I no longer felt sorry for him. But we still weren't getting any water. And that was the overriding concern and so the dufuss was soon forgotten and then it happened.

A thing that hardly anyone over the decades and even centuries of military warfare history ever gets to witness. And would probably be better off not to. The navy corpsman, who had become increasingly frazzled and desperate in his ongoing attempts to save the lives of the heat stroke casualties walked briskly and directly up to the Captain in charge of our part of the operation. They stopped and squared off a foot apart. Just a few feet from where I was standing in the hot baking sun on the bald peak of a jagged mountain in north western South Vietnam. Just a stones throw from the eastern border of Laos. And the Corpsman looks straight at the Captain's face.

The Captain, who was still working our tired asses to beat the band, and this is what the Corpsman said: "Sir, with all due respect, under Article..." *...such and such and so and so...*"as the senior Medical Officer..." *...in charge of the physical welfare of the personnel on this operation and because of the critical nature of the medical emergency conditions we are faced with and the undeniable and immanent prospect of certain fatalities...*"I do hereby assume Command."

And he did. The Captain just glared at him! Not a word. And the whole world just sort of stood completely still. The Captain, who really looked like he was going to explode, turned abruptly and walked about as fast as humanly possible without actually running over to the guy with the radio. And the Captain practically rips it out of the radioman's hands and cranks it up and barks out, no yells out, some kind of angry command into the hand mike, with his apoplectic face and bulging eyeballs glaring out into the uncaring sky. And this is no shit. Within no more than fifteen or twenty minutes this little Plexiglas bubble shaped Bell two seat Helicopter comes out of nowhere. It sets down like a bumblebee on a Cornflower and the Captain leaps aboard. Without so much as a *fare-thee-well*. He didn't even wave goodbye.

He was gone.

They didn't leave so much as a drop of water. We weren't sorry to see him go. That Corpsman had balls. It was unbelievable to see and hear what he did and said. Before that day was over after at least three days and nights without a resupply, the first chopper approached our aerial position. It had no intention of landing. Instead it was carrying on the end of at least a hundred feet of rope a pallet of about a ton of green steel canisters of water.

The weight of the load, together with the hurried pace of the chopper as it banked in toward our position, caused the pallet of water canisters to swing erratically, which caused the chopper to heave back and forth uncontrollably. So they cut the rope. The load was coming down. It was coming down all two thousand pounds of it at a high rate of speed. And it was coming down directly in my direction. And this is when I did something that had enormous consequences for a guy I didn't even know. A guy they called: "Tex."

Tex was a big very muscular black guy and he was one of the grunts. He didn't exactly look too much like a cowboy so I figured he was probably just from Texas. Anyway, he never so much as said boo to me even though he was camped just about six to eight feet away from me and we were both of us under our respective suspended ponchos in the trees at the edge of the perimeter, hiding from the sun. Only Tex was sound asleep. Probably back in Houston in an air-conditioned R and B Bar with a tall Gin Fizz and a lovely long legged lady with almond shaped eyes whose name was Cocoa or Brandy or something like that and all I did was shout very loud above the coughing sound of the passing overhead chopper:

"Tex! Move! Get outta there!"

Or something just like that and about one tenth of a second after Tex's heavy dream locked eyelids popped open and he sees me gesticulating wildly with my hands and arms, he rolls out from under his poncho and: "BOOM!" The pallet, the ton of green steel water canisters and all of the additional force and weight caused by the chopper banking, the load swinging outward like a water skier, flanking out when the speedboat takes a sharp turn in the opposing direction, it all comes down square on the poncho where Tex just a millisecond before was under, back in the World, dreaming of God only knows what. He would have been just a black and red smudge pressed unknowingly into the hot red Vietnamese soil, on the top of a mountain whose name I never knew. And he would have never even known it happened.

It took twenty or thirty years before it dawned on me that Tex didn't say a word to me about it. Not a word. That's just how things were. And it don't mean nothing. But somehow or another

I've got to think that it had to mean something to Tex. At least I hope so.

Oh yeah, there was a lot of other stuff that happened out there. I always wondered what happened after I left. After they brought the guns out there and they brought in the cannon cockers. The arty guys that would man the howitzers for weeks or months at a stretch.

I know I had a real bad feeling about that place. I didn't envy the people who were going to be staying there. If we were able to scale the mountain with eighty pound packs, so would a battalion of lightly clad NVA. And it was their turf.

It was like floating on a leaky raft in shark infested water.

Shit.

I remember watching a chopper across the valley lower a rope down along the steep slope of a neighboring mountain and two Marines helped secure a third into the suspended sling. It looked to me that they were out there alone, in the middle of Nowhere. A three man recon team that had run into some kind of bad luck in a bad place and they were getting one wounded out. Then the remaining two would be on the run. And to call in the medivac chopper was putting them at even greater risk. It was like painting a big red arrow in the sky that was pointed down directly at their exact location. A big arrow that was making a lot of noise.

You really had to admire those guys. The small recognizance teams and the forward observers, FO's, who went out there alone and called in the coordinates for the artillery batteries. And I recalled the story an FO had told me back in camp. What he called: "Hell's Alley."

He said that when a forward observer or a recon team was trapped and surrounded with no avenue of escape, he or they would call in their last hope: *Hell's Alley*. And the artillery battery would fire their rounds so as to create a circle of exploding ordinance around the desperate Marines. Then on the designated side of the circle create an alley of descending artillery rounds to provide just the slightest possibility of successful egress from their otherwise doomed position.

Of course the shrapnel alone could cut them to ribbons. At such close quarters. And it had to be perfect.

Just the slightest miscalculation on the part of the artillery or the caller and it was all over. It was almost too amazing to be true. But a lot of stuff was like that. Too much stuff to ever be told. And I wondered what it was like to be lost out there without any witnesses. Completely alone. No one even to tell your story. And that's the sorrow. Below and beyond all the pain and loss, is to be unknown. Lost. In the bush. In the jungle. In the everglades:

"If the skeeters don't get you then the gators will."*

And the *skeeters* were the bullets and the hot jagged shards of shrapnel buzzing madly through the chaotic and supercharged atmosphere, seeking the warm soft flesh of the entrapped Marines.

*(EVERGLADES, by the Kingston Trio, © 1960.)

206

The *gators*, the NVA, encircling, encroaching and relentlessly pressing inward towards the center for the kill. Or even worse, to capture alive the object or objects of their ruthless desire.

Unless everything worked perfectly. Eventually, the sad and gloomy reality of these brave men's sacrifice would be recorded in some dusty ledger, simply and efficiently as KIA/BNR: *Killed In Action / Body Not Returned.* Or the more ambiguous and untidy acronym MIA: *Missing In Action.*

Oh what a lucky sucker I was. To be in my boots and not in theirs. Do you think I didn't know that? Do you think I didn't feel the shame? The shame to survive and to have had it easy? *Easy.* Compared to what might have been.

Oh but I did and I still do. But that's not really so much to give is it?

The hovering chopper lifted the wounded Marine up into its belly and was gone. The jungle closed back up again on those that remained behind.

THE YEAR OF THE RAT

Chopper door gunner

Grunts on *Operation Campbell Streamer*

Mountain shot of Valley - My buddy Chapman from 1/13

Author's foot from under poncho - The author at dinner

THE YEAR OF THE RAT

"I'm Going Home"

The navy guy came out of the Quonset Hut door after everybody had been taken inside. Lifted up off their sawhorses and whisked away into the labyrinth of Quonset Huts that were connected in such a fashion, that the surgical field hospital on the tarmac of the airfield on the outskirts of Danang looked like a train wreck. And he picked up a hose. Just like he'd done it a million times before. So casual. And he directed the flow of water from left to right, left to right, starting from the corner of the large cement slab, working the pool of fresh blood into a crimson wave underneath and between the long rows of sawhorses arranged like a company of cavalry steeds. About 75 to 100 of them. Spaced apart so as to hold the stretchers which held the fallen warriors whose blood had spilled profusely, as if from a torn and broken collective heart, onto the concrete surface below.

I watched him wash the blood away.

Sitting back down on a wooden bench outside of the triage area after having just finished helping carry the wounded Marines on stretchers from the medivac helicopters. They had come in and landed like a swarm of manic locusts. Each of the two or three times I was sent down there to see a doctor, this would happen. And I felt a little bit indigenous. Like a native. Like a gook. When I helped carry the stretchers from the choppers over to the sawhorses because I would be wearing shower shoes instead of jungle boots. And as I ran along on my end of the stretchers the thongs would flip flop, flip flop and the sound would accompany the "phu-phu-phu" of the rotor blades of the incoming and idling aerial ambulances. The medivac helicopters.

And the Vietnamese, the locals that I generally saw, wore sandals. *Ho Chi Minhs*. They were usually made out of tire treads and inner tubes. I had a pair of them myself. But I was wearing shower shoes and I was at the hospital because of severe jungle rot. It had pretty much affixed itself to my entire body. And when your feet became so infected that to continue wearing boots would eventually disable you and if you were lucky enough that someone actually gave a damn, you might be issued a *Shower Shoe Chit*. A piece of paper signed by a doctor that authorized you to temporarily go without boots and to go about your business in thongs.

And another thing that was kind of troubling, was that my eyes had begun to seal shut. From the secretions and puss that would dry out and harden into a glue that would seal my eyelids together. When I was asleep. And what I would do is make sure I had a canteen close by where I could reach it in the dark and I would rub water into my eyes to break them free.

As I sat there on the bench waiting for the wounded to be treated and for the blood to be washed away, I felt...like I was insignificant. But at least I helped carry them.

Carry them from the choppers. To the sawhorses. And I didn't mind waiting. Sitting on a bench. In the sun. Alone. Hell, I didn't care if they never called me. It gave me time. Alone. Away from any hassles. You wouldn't believe how rare that was. But what was really on my mind was that one guy. He was about three or four stretchers ahead of me. And on that particular lap, I was holding the rear handles of a stretcher and as we were trucking them around the open compound, from the helicopters to the legion of waiting sawhorses, that one guy did an incredible thing. A memorable thing. The kind of thing that even made the crazy doctor have to take a backseat. The doc I was thinking about right before the last batch of medivac choppers came in.

I was thinking about my last encounter with him back at camp. When I decided to stop taking the pills. Now I know that this was no big deal in the great scheme of things. And I already said how I felt insignificant. And I knew all along that: "It don't mean nothin".

This is what I was thinking right before the medivac choppers came in.

The Doc had put me on an "experimental treatment". Some three or four months before. For the jungle rot. The way it was explained to me was that every six months every cell in the human body would die off and be reborn, so that in essence after six months, every cell in the human body would die off and a new one would be born to take its place.

Consequently, after six months, you would have a whole new body and the drug would effectively kill off the infections that were causing the lesions on my skin and the oozing discharges from my eyes and various other areas. It all sounded reasonable enough to me. Until one day with not a particular thought in my head, I opened up a new box of the prescribed drug. For the first time I opened it from the bottom. Took out the bottle of pills. For some unknown reason, I extracted and unfolded and read the little pamphlet which had previously gone without my notice. Concealed as it was surreptitiously in the bottom of the box. I didn't need to get to the fine print and the technical medical mumbo jumbo below the heading and the first sentence, because it was the capitalized heading and the following line that, like a sudden lightning bolt, caught and seized my singular attention.

This is what it said:

"CAUTION - HEAVY DOSAGE OF STEROIDS. DO NOT USE FOR A PROLONGED PERIOD OF TIME."

Now like I said: "I ain't no Einstein." Nor, am I a Ph.D. But as soon as I read the word *Steroids* an electrical current went straight from my bulging brain to my instantly constricted testicles. I knew right then and there, at the ripe old age of nineteen years old, that I would never ever be able to have children. And I became enraged. Engulfed with pathological fury. Ready to explode. My hot and blistered brain ticking like a live pinless grenade. And it just so happened that right at that time, or shortly thereafter and one cannot tell time when in a state of rage, that the doctor just happened to be in town.

In fact, he was right there in that little shack up on the hill of the 26th Marines. The very shack whose rickety door I practically broke off the hinges as I burst inside, a raving madman, demanding with extreme prejudice an immediate consultation with the good doctor. As soon as he came from the back of the hooch to the wooden counter inside the front door where I was waiting, I screamed: "Can these pills make you sterile!?" And it was at that exact moment that I noticed there was something really odd about that doctor. He did not look right. In fact he suddenly looked to me completely crazed. With a *maniacal expression*. And he started gesticulating wildly, his arms waving about him as he lunged forward toward me as if he was going to come right over the counter. The counter which I was suddenly glad was there.

In a voice that I can only describe and what has always reminded me of and has long *echoed* ever since the very first moment I heard it, off the walls of the long dark hallways of my memory, as the very same voice employed by the Walt Disney character *Goofy* and it went something like this: "*Wa ahell, aha aha aha, wa, ahell, ahell, wa ah guess so.*"

He looked and sounded like he had to be on some kind of hallucinating drugs. Either that or I was. In any event, without much hesitation and fit to be tied and at that point perhaps we both should have been, I flung the canister of pills with maximum force and velocity down upon the counter and it exploded like a satchel charge. Sending sprays of shrapnel pills all over the mad doctor and the surrounding area. And with the sound of his hysterical rant roiling in my incensed brain, I stormed out through the door of the medical shack. Hinges be damned. I didn't look back.

But I didn't blame the doctor for being crazy. Sitting on the bench by the Quonset Hut Hospital. Watching the guy with the hose washing away the ever flowing crimson tide of fresh blood.

So casual.

All you had to do was look at what we brought in on the stretchers. Rested on the tired sawhorses. Like offerings. That the harried docs could not refuse.

And these gifts were brought to them every day, night, week and month. Like a continuous procession. Without end.

218

The common currency of the offerings was the blood. A seemingly endless supply. No, I didn't blame the doc for being crazy. And I suspect that I was some kind of comic relief to him.

Still I always wondered what the hell those pills had done to me. And I never took them again.

Then it happened. The guy three or four stretchers before me. He blew all my self-centered reverie away. Just like a 122 millimeter rocket had hit dead center on the middle of my self-absorbed thoughts.

Kaboom!

And this is all he did. I had seen when we unloaded him from the medivac chopper that his legs were shot up. But it looked to me like he would keep them. He just raised up on the stretcher on his left elbow. Flung his right arm and fist straight up into the air and you had to wonder, what the hell he was thinking. Who he was really talking to, when he said, when he yelled, at the top of his lungs and I swear, every single lost and lonely soul on every hill, valley and rice paddy in Vietnam and throughout Southeast Asia, could hear him. And maybe even in other parts of the World.

Could hear what I heard.

Just three plain but infinitely meaningful words. Wrenched from the guts of just another wounded and surviving Marine. Fresh from the battle.

And this is all he said:

"I'M GOING HOOOOooommmmeeee!"

...to the World

What can I say? What can any of us say? There were too many thoughts. Too much had happened. You couldn't tell it all. And I didn't want to. The only thing that anyone wanted was to just go home. Go the hell home!

Curl up in a soft bed and maybe even before that, to take a long warm bath. Just wash away everything in the big porcelain bowl that for so long was just a beautiful and comforting dream.

You can't imagine. To take a real bath. The warm water rising up around your tired body. Like a protective cocoon. A chrysalis. But you never thought that you would unfold into some kind of beautiful butterfly. No. You would be lucky just to survive.

My mother's bathtub in a low rent apartment was enough. At least for the first night. God! You just wouldn't believe it. The warm luxurious water slowly rising and covering my tired naked body. It felt so much like an out of body experience. Like heaven...

After that and sleeping on her couch, I had bad dreams. I shook for at least two months before I left off on my own. Just to survive. But I was lucky. I had legs. In fact I was never even wounded. No visible scars. Except for a little piece of shrapnel that worked its way out of the back of my head about three months after I came home. But I didn't tell anybody about it. What for? It didn't mean nothing. Who the hell wanted to hear about it? Nobody. No, you kept it to yourself.

And that was all right. I didn't want to tell anybody anyway. You just snuck back into the World. Like a thief. And that is just exactly what Sandy and I did.

We got onto that big ass airplane in Danang when nobody was looking. A DC something or other commercial airliner. With stewardesses and everything. But I don't remember anything after we took off. I do remember though that it seemed as if nothing had even touched Sandy. He was beautiful. I really mean it. When we walked onto that plane you could just tell that he would have no trouble merging back into the World.

Well I do remember one thing. When we first took off and lifted up off the runway there was dead silence. It stayed like that. Until the Captain came over the intercom and said something about leaving the territorial airspace of Vietnam, or something like that and everybody just gasped and went crazy. But it didn't last long.

It was like everyone was holding their breath. Expecting, really expecting, that we would take that final rocket. Blown away on liftoff.

Then the movies began. Not a Hollywood movie. There wasn't a movie screen on the plane. There were just the movies in our brains. For each guy sitting on that plane there was an individual movie. Spliced and edited over a thirteen month period of time. Not just any time, but prime time. I was nineteen when I came back from Vietnam. Like many others. Everything was weighted when you were in your teens.

Think about it. Your first kiss. Your prom. Your date at the drive-in movie. Everybody was thinking about the things they had left behind. Back in the World. A girlfriend. A dog. A little sister. A mom. Or a bed. A soft cool comforting bed with no one else around. Not a barracks or a hooch. Not a bunker or a trench. Just something clean and safe. And quiet. That's the way you wanted it to be. And right from that thought...right from those memories...the frames as they reeled by soundlessly inside your brain would change.

From the past achingly longed for memories and future hoped for dreams. To the Rat. The Rat of War. The careless soulless hungry pitiless Rat of War. The dead and beady eyes. Right there in front of your face.

Staring.

And the Rat remained. He was there before you and he was there after you left. Like the **"*Phuc Yew Lizard*"**. So named because that is the sound it would make. Sitting up high in the rafters of your hooch. Mocking and taunting you with its condescending call:

"Phuc yew, phuc yew, phuc yew...."

The Rat fed off the war. It grew strong off the mess and the death. The Rat thrived. And it mocked you with its cold clammy indifference to your hapless plight.

And the Rat was patient.

It knew that sooner or later it would have its meal. All it had to do was wait. And as we lifted up off of the tarmac, the red ground and the impossibly green and carnivorous creature below, into the incredibly blue and ethereal heavens above:

I knew.

Just as sure as the frame in front of my face. That the Rat would remain and that I was taking it with me. Just like *Sandy*. And *Tater*. And *Johnny the New Guy*. And *all of the others*.

It was a full ride.

THE YEAR OF THE RAT

EPILOG

We ask you to forgive the author of this book. He didn't have a choice. He didn't want to write our stories. But we never really gave him a choice.

We just kept working on him. Year after year. And finally we wore him down. Before he forgot. Before we were forgotten. And we showed him no mercy. We really worked him over.

In fact, we played these stories over and over again and again in his head. Until he just couldn't take it anymore. It's not his fault. It really isn't.

Forever young,
Sandy, Johnny the New Guy,
Tator & the Rest...

THE YEAR OF THE RAT

AFTERWARD

(Oops, there goes my hooch again)

Oh, I almost forgot. Remember how I saw those ***slithering human shapes*** up on the side of the hill? At night through the ***Starlight Scope***? How I saw them two nights in a row and reported it both times and even tried to take some guys and go up there?

Well, after I went home and had a thirty day leave, I had to go back in for two more months and I spent the last two months in San Diego at MCRD, the ***Marine Corps Recruit Depot***. Where I went through boot camp. And when I was there I just happened to meet up with my old First Sergeant. Top Sergeant Williams. And he was quite a sight. Even after six months or so, there he was and his right arm was sticking up at a *right angle* like he was perpetually stopping traffic. But what had happened is that the First Sergeant, who some people had bitched about because he held weapons inspections at least once a week and was very serious about them, had leapt into a hole where three young Marines were mortally wounded. He tried with all his might to save them. Firing his M16. Until a Chicom Grenade neutralized him and tore his right arm to ribbons.

Try as he did to save them, the three Marines died from their wounds, but First Sergeant Williams survived. And there he was. An old black Marine who had worked his way up the ranks over a period of many years. A tough old salt. And he was right. The discipline he practiced on us was not lost on me. I didn't bitch. I always knew he was right. And seeing him there at MCRD in San Diego was refreshing to my soul. With his right arm sticking up in a cast at a comical perfect right angle like a stop-traffic sign, he spoke to me. He recognized me. And he spoke to me like a man. Like a fellow Marine.

AFTERWARD

I can't remember exactly what he said to me, but I do remember him telling me that about a week or so after I left Vietnam, my hooch was hit and blown up again. Maybe just a few days after I left. And I knew for sure where the mortar or mortars came from. Right up on that hill where I had seen the slithering shapes.

But it don't mean nothing. It could have been anybody. In that hooch. At that time.

It just wasn't me.

THE YEAR OF THE RAT

Made in the USA